Unwin Education Books: 3

PHYSICAL EDUCATION FOR TEACHING

Unwin Education Books

Series Editor: Ivor Morrish, BD, BA, DIP. ED. (London), BA (Bristol)

1. EDUCATION SINCE 1800
   IVOR MORRISH
2. MORAL DEVELOPMENT
   WILLIAM KAY
3. PHYSICAL EDUCATION FOR TEACHING
   BARBARA CHURCHER
4. THE BACKGROUND OF IMMIGRANT CHILDREN
   IVOR MORRISH
5. ORGANISING AND INTEGRATING THE INFANT DAY
   JOY TAYLOR
6. PHILOSOPHY OF EDUCATION: AN INTRODUCTION
   HARRY SCHOFIELD
7. ASSESSMENT AND TESTING: AN INTRODUCTION
   HARRY SCHOFIELD
8. EDUCATION: ITS NATURE AND PURPOSE
   M. V. C. JEFFREYS
9. LEARNING IN THE PRIMARY SCHOOL
   KENNETH HASLAM
10. SOCIOLOGY OF EDUCATION: AN INTRODUCTION
    IVOR MORRISH
11. FIFTY YEARS OF FREEDOM
    RAY HEMMINGS
12. DEVELOPING A CURRICULUM
    AUDREY AND HOWARD NICHOLLS
13. TEACHER EDUCATION AND CULTURAL CHANGE
    H. DUDLEY PLUNKETT AND J. LYNCH

Unwin Education Books: 3
Series Editor: Ivor Morrish

Physical Education for Teaching

BARBARA CHURCHER
Principal Lecturer in Physical Education
Newcastle-upon-Tyne College of Education

London
GEORGE ALLEN AND UNWIN LTD
RUSKIN HOUSE MUSEUM STREET

First published in 1927 under the title
Physical Training, Games and Athletics in Schools
Completely revised 1971
Second Revised Edition

© George Allen & Unwin Ltd 1971, 1972

ISBN 0 04 371024 7 *Paper*

Printed in Great Britain
in 10 point Times Roman
by Redwood Press Limited
Trowbridge, Wiltshire

Preface

One of the difficulties for students is to relate theory to practical activities and *vice versa*, and an effort has been made to illustrate the one by the other throughout. Because, however, every teacher is creative in his own way, it is not supposed that the practical examples will be other than indicative of possible and differing lines of development.

A second consideration lies in the difference of approach between the expressive and functional aspects of movement. Expressive movement should give emotional and aesthetic satisfaction and be an outlet for creativeness as are poetry and music. Physical skills need to be learnt and expertise acquired *before* they can be used creatively. The teacher needs to be clear throughout about these two aspects of his work. Young children should not be conscious of any dichotomy but older children, who want to be proficient at skills, appreciate it increasingly and should grow to understand the values of both these aspects of physical education.

I am greatly indebted to my colleague, Mrs Joyce Lambert, lecturer in dance at Newcastle College of Education, for her kindness in critical evaluation and for providing material on dance.

The teacher is referred to as 'he' throughout this book but clearly wherever applicable the masculine should be taken to include the feminine gender.

1971   B. C.

Acknowledgements

The photographs in this section showing children working were taken by Mr J. Leslie Otley, A.R.P.S., at the following schools:
Barley Mow Learner Pool, Co. Durham;
Gosforth East Infant and Junior Schools, Northumberland;
Elgin Secondary Technical School, Gateshead;
Greenwell Secondary Modern School, Gateshead.

The author gratefully acknowledges the co-operation of Mr Otley and the head teachers, staff and children at these schools.

'I would have the disposition of his limbs formed at the same time with his mind. . . .' – *Montaigne, sixteenth century*

The changes that are evident in present-day physical education are not the result of new and startling theories, but are due to the recurrence of three educational ideas which have acquired new emphasis from modern psychology. The three are: the wholeness of the child, the individuality of the child, and the effectiveness of activity and experience in the learning process.

Contents

Preface   *page*   7

1. General Aims – the Teacher's Approach   13
2. Ways of Learning – Immediate Aims – Teaching Technique   16
3. The Scope – Laban's Principles   22
4. The Primary Programme – Development of a Lesson Plan – Clothing for Physical Activity – Preparation of the Hall   26
5. The Primary Programme (continued) – Gymnastics   30
6. The Primary Programme (continued) – The Gymnastic Lesson Plan (Stages I and II)   34
7. The Primary Programme (continued) – The Climax of the Gymnastic Lesson – Group Practices – Organization of Apparatus – Group Leaders – Safety   52
8. The Primary Programme (continued) – Progression in Gymnastics further up the Primary School   57
9. The Primary Programme (continued) – Play Interests at Different Ages – Play Theories – Values of Play   63
10. The Primary Programme (continued) – Games in Primary Education (Stages I, II and III)   70
11. The Primary Programme (continued) – Swimming in Primary Education (Stages I and II)   86
12. The Primary Programme (continued) – Dance in Primary Education – Body Awareness – Spatial Awareness – Dynamic Awareness – The Sixteen Basic Movement Themes – Stimuli in Dance   100
13. Further Considerations of Teaching Technique – 'Process and Product' in Physical Education – the Teacher's Rôle – Presentation of Work – Discipline – Observation – Demonstrations – Movement Quality and Standard of Work – Progression – Accidents – Exemption from Physical Activity – Posture   117
14. The Secondary Programme – The Scope – A Basic Course – Gymnastics – Games Training (Stages I and II) – Swimming – Dance – Athletics   130
15. The Teacher – Educational Effects of Physical Education – Transfer of Training   159

List of Reference Books 162
List of Equipment Manufacturers 164
Index 165

Illustrations

Plates (between pages 80 and 81)
1. *Top:* Travelling about the floor using hands and feet, (*bottom*) balancing on part of the body.
2. *Left:* Finding places on the apparatus where the body can hang and stretch, (*right*) the body can hang and curl too.
3. *Left:* Feet can help hands to hang, (*above*) other parts of the body can support the weight on apparatus.
4. *Right:* Large parts can bear the body weight, (*below*) small parts too.
5. *Left:* Travelling up and down the square ladder, (*right*) balance on or over the apparatus using other parts to help hands and feet.
6. *Top:* 'Swimming' with a polystyrene float, (*bottom*) free play.
7. *Top:* Hands – (*right*) can dance.
8. *Left:* A spiky dance, (*below*) dancing in a group with a percussion instrument.
9. *Left:* Contrasting shapes, (*right*) high and low.
10. *Left:* A small shape, (*right*) exploding!
11. *Top left:* Hands and feet travelling along a form, (*top right*) bearing a partner's weight, (*bottom*) two make a gap the third travels through.
12 and 13. *Left:* Travelling about the floor emphasizing feet high, (*right and opposite page*) elevation and contrast in shape in jumping off a form.
14. Using parts of the body to balance and travel on form, beams and floor.
15. *Top:* Elbows move near to the body, (*bottom*) work with a partner at a medium level.
16. *Top:* Using of hands at high level – (*bottom*) in preparation for a group dance.

Figures
1. An analysis of body movement   23
2. An arrangement of small apparatus to develop work in six groups   44
3. An arrangement of large apparatus, supplemented by small, to develop work in five groups   45
4. An arrangement of large apparatus to develop work in five groups   46
5. An arrangement of apparatus to form a route for group work   49
6. Axes of movement in personal space   103
7. Diagram showing the build-up of effort actions from combinations of effort elements   104
8. Graph showing the progression of the sixteen movement themes for ages 5 to 18 years   108

Chapter 1

General Aims – The Teacher's Approach

The general aim of physical education, as of all education, should be 'the harmonious development of the child's body and mind'. A teacher concerns himself with aims, methods, procedures and apparatus, but his greatest concern is with the children for whom, with others, he takes responsibility. He may be a teacher of physical education, divinity, history or science, but his primary responsibility is to help children to grow and develop as human beings. Though he cannot at all times keep in mind this development of personalities, the determining factor in all his decisions should be the nature, potentialities and needs of the children.

Children's Natural Activity and Interests

Whether a child goes to school or not, his waking life will be one of vigorous physical and mental activity. It is the work of the school to see that this activity is both satisfying to the child and also a means of growth and development.

By nature the child's most general urge is to be active; in fact his constant activity is the way in which this urge shows itself. He needs activity, both physical and mental, especially as his physical and intellectual qualities are the major determinants of his personality. His physical education is one way of supplying both and the present-day approach gives him the physical satisfaction of movements of various qualities and the mental satisfaction of creative activity.

THE TEACHER'S APPROACH

As the teacher of physical education shares with his colleagues the responsibility for the development of the children as personalities he must see his contribution in relation to the whole work of the school. *The trend of education as a whole has altered.* The aim was formerly utilitarian, to supply knowledge and teach skills to fit the individual for work and livelihood. No planned allowance was made for emotional development. If the children's emotions or urges were satisfied this was incidental.

The development of psychology and, thus, of *insight into motives* has made it clear that actions in life are not guided by reason and logic alone, but rather by our emotions. We may have an intellectual conviction that we should sleep with a window open, or wash regularly, or maintain a good posture, but unless we have an emotional urge to do so we shall not consistently do such things. Hence the approach to education for all children, though perhaps in more obvious ways in younger children, now follows the pattern of their developing interests rather than a logical textbook exposition. We work harder and with greater urge to succeed, to perfect and reach our objective, if what we do we enjoy doing and consider worth while. Children's effort is most effective when it is sustained by some urge within themselves, by curiosity, interest or the urge to express or do.

At no time is the teacher more purposefully and more profitably occupied than when he is, by suggestion and encouragement, ensuring valuable learning from the children's self-chosen and, to the children, self-directed activity. By this approach he ensures that every individual child, not just a few, makes progress and achieves satisfaction and confidence. If the children express what is asked, at their own rate and in their own way, they do not feel in the wrong or left behind as in competitive work. This is the more so when each child realizes that he has some contribution to make to the class through being asked to demonstrate if a type of movement which he can show is required.

In physical education the teacher no longer tries to help the child to develop by treating him as a mechanical object that responds automatically, unchangingly and inevitably to orders, as a machine does to the man at the controls. The child, unlike the machine, has mental powers similar in kind, though as yet less developed, to those of the teacher. He has vigorous urges, strong feelings and interests; many of them are inborn and common to all people. The teacher of physical education makes use of these mental qualities.

Children's Likenesses and Differences

A teacher's study of children must be twofold. On the one hand he must know the *common characteristics* of children at various ages and stages of growth, as for example that all small children are self-centred. On the other hand he needs to study the *individual differences* between the members of a group or class, for instance that some like the limelight while others are shy and retiring, some are easily discouraged while others are impetuous and tend to take risks readily, some approach a problem slowly and methodically while others are quick and careless, some are tall and strong in contrast to smaller and weaker children of the same age.

Thus the teacher's knowledge of common characteristics makes him able to provide suitable material, apparatus and organization. His awareness of the individual nature of children prepares him to accept that each child has his *own characteristic way of moving and his own movement potential.*

Although the work is child-centred, the teacher is the essential force in the scheme, for apart from planning he must observe, analyse, coach, suggest and encourage. Only thus will his aim of helping each child to fulfil his movement potential be achieved, only thus will each child discover the essence of his own natural way of moving and be educated physically by having his experience widened to include the movement characteristics of other children.

Chapter 2

Ways of Learning – Immediate Aims – Teaching Technique

WAYS OF LEARNING

Children learn in different ways according to their individual nature and the stage through which they are passing. The teacher needs to be aware that younger children, the timid and unsure, the class which is trying new work and apparatus, will first approach learning through *exploration*. This stage cannot be hurried, especially for young children who learn by exploring tirelessly both their own powers and the challenge of their environment. If skills and techniques are introduced at this point, movement loses spontaneity, becomes stereotyped and unimaginative. On the other hand, if exploration is allowed to continue for too long without some guidance, children become bored and lose their sense of purpose and effort; thus the work tends to revert in character to the 'play' of the nursery stage.

As a result of his exploration the child should be observed to be *creating* movements which the teacher will encourage him to repeat, for *repetition* is important in gaining mastery over his body as a basis for confidence in attempting more difficult work and apparatus in the future.

Further stages of learning are seen in the *selection* the child makes of the movement or skill appropriate to the task set by the teacher. He needs help to modify and clarify his movement in order to make his solution more appropriate and the final *application* of it more effective.

Playlike Activities

There is no doubt that children learn a great deal, naturally, through spontaneous and undirected play. The body language of such play is instinctive and, left to himself, the child will walk, run, skip, jump, roll, slide, swing, spin, balance and climb. These activities will provide the best foundation for his physical education if the teacher can appreciate their possibilities and evolve a teaching technique which ensures that they do not degenerate into mere barren repetition or retain the apparently aimless nature of nursery play. Before looking at technique, however, it is important to state the immediate aims of a physical education lesson of any type.

IMMEDIATE AIMS

What benefits should children gain through their physical education lessons? Broadly speaking we should aim for:

1 *Exertion:* vigorous exercise which disturbs breathing. Especially at the primary stage it is vital that we satisfy the child's appetite for activity. Endurance, perhaps, is not so important in the early stages, but the development of stamina should be part of our ultimate aim.

2 *Enjoyment and satisfaction.* Innate in the child is the enjoyment of movement; he communicates, he expresses wishes, needs and emotions through this medium. It should not be difficult to harness what is so necessary and enjoyable to him. Children's enjoyment is, in itself, worth while but our success in this direction provides the *motivation* for further interest and participation, making the fulfilment of this aim more than ever important.

3 *Acquisition of skills.* The growing child appreciates the need for skill and is, in fact, deprived without the development of his natural maturation skills. His future versatility depends on the wide range of skills made possible for him.

4 *Strong physique.* The whole body must be involved in the vigorous pursuit of motor skills so that a balanced development results. We should also be concerned with the range of movement in the joints as mobility tends to deteriorate with age. Concern with postural faults, in children generally, would appear unnecessary if this aim were fully implemented.

5 *Self expression.* Children are not adults in miniature and their ways of expressing themselves should not be moulded to conform with adult standards. Opportunities for expression of liveliness, feeling and form need not necessarily be associated with uncontrolled egotistical behaviour.

6 *Social training.* The physical situation presents suitable opportunities for fostering attitudes of friendly co-operation, fair play and sharing.

The achievement of these aims seems to lie with the teacher's recognition of the individual – each child is different in attitude, ability, capacity, body physique, rate of movement – and concern for the individual pupil's happiness. Both matters demand the right environment, a learning situation which is a happy one, based on mutual respect between pupil and teacher, plus the interest the latter inspires in the child. Furthermore, the teacher must recognize *individual effort and approach* and no longer look for a set answer or arbitrary standard. The present-day approach is psychological rather than purely anatomical. Thus the teacher, instead of imposing carefully graded exercises with anticipated progressions, must set himself to draw out each individual child to pursue his own movement interests. Exploration and invention take time and if children are rushed on from one activity to another without time to settle down and concentrate on the task, they cannot become absorbed in what they are doing. Unless they know that they will be given time to experiment, they cannot try out new ways of doing things or work out an idea. Thus the child should, in general, be allowed *to work at his own pace*, though giving him time to work in this way does not leave him in a vacuum, for the teacher meanwhile helps him with suggestions and encouragement.

If, in response to the teacher's challenge, the child is to have room to experiment in his own way, and if the teacher needs to see and analyse each child's efforts, *free spacing* provides a more suitable learning situation than the formality and restriction of four lines. Individual differences, especially the physical differences of size and shape, will also preclude work in unison. To satisfy the sheer appetite for activity there can be no waiting for turns.

Informality

The *activity method* or the *informal* approach is suitable to our greater awareness of how children learn. *Informality* must not, however, be regarded as a loosely-woven mesh, but as a supporting framework made up of a number of teaching techniques. Good teaching and informality are not mutually exclusive but, rather, complementary.

TEACHING TECHNIQUE

To achieve results the teacher will base his teaching on the ingredients of:

1 *A conversational approach* based on the giving of tasks or challenges to be answered in movement. Education in terms of movement, like that of language, aims at increasing the child's vocabulary. In the case of movement, he learns mainly by trying for himself, but his understanding is given form by exchanging ideas with the teacher and by responding, in movement mainly but sometimes in words, to his skilful use of the 'question and answer technique'.

Further examples of the conversational approach are seen in the presentation of stimuli to inspire imagery and creativity (most appropriate to dance), and a sparing use of 'watch me and you do'. The latter should only be used when the children, having been allowed to 'have a go', show themselves to be lacking ideas. It can also, of course, introduce the demonstration of a specific skill.

The conversational manner should not be thought of as a continuous and aimless narrative – indeed this cannot be the case in a lesson meant for children's activity.

2 *The command – response method* which is not entirely precluded by the conversational approach. Children may need, and enjoy, the occasional stimulus of a command which calls for an alert response. Such training may also be necessary as part of the teacher's provision for safety, and 'Stop' is certainly a direction that is sometimes needed.

3 *Copying and imitation.* Teacher demonstration has been briefly mentioned in 1 above, but it is well known that children learn much from one another by either unconsciously copying or deliberately imitating a demonstration which the teacher asks one or more members of the class to give. The whole question of demonstrations will be dealt with more fully later in the book, but it can be stressed here that they should always follow children's own attempts to answer a challenge and then should, in turn, be followed by further efforts.

4 *Observation and analysis of individual efforts.* At first the teacher needs to observe differences; one child is relatively slow, another likes twisting movements, a third prefers light, quick action, and a fourth chooses strong movements requiring a great deal of energy. The children work experimentally within their preferences, the teacher guiding each child to find his natural solutions to the tasks set, then proceeding to widen his movement experience and heighten his performance. The latter process is very much dependent on *coaching*, especially those coaching points given to the individual child after observing and analysing his performance. Common class coaching points may be observed if the teacher, having given the challenge, stands aside and watches while the whole class makes an attempt. The anticipation and preparation of suitable coaching points come more easily to the teacher who has personally experienced the kind of work being asked of the class.

5 *Suitable voice and manner.* Inherent in the process of *guidance* mentioned in the paragraph above is the teacher's manner of quiet praise and encouragement, sometimes stimulating but not consistently over-stimulating and brisk, as may at one time have been felt necessary. This unobtrusive teacher-control allows the children freedom to think and work and gives more confidence than teacher-dominance.

Careful Preparation

Fundamental to good teaching is careful preparation based on the needs, ability and previous experience of the class. Present-day physical education is not concerned with a list of things to be done, but there must be a basis on which to build. Within any lesson, the most important concern for the teacher is the reaction of the children. This can only be dealt with adequately if the teacher has confidence in his preparation of carefully selected and suitable material and his organization of apparatus and group work.

Such preparation is of two kinds, which could be thought of as long and short term.

Long-term preparation involves the making of a *scheme of work* to last a few weeks, say a half or even a whole term. Only by planning ahead in this way can the teacher ensure a logical and purposeful development of work and the inclusion of all those ingredients necessary to the child's education in movement.

A scheme should give all the necessary and linked information about the class and the work to be attempted, and could be based on the answering of the following questions:

1 How many children, boys and/or girls?
2 How old are they?
3 What facilities and apparatus are available for the activity?
4 How much time is available for the work planned?
5 What is the specific purpose of the scheme?
6 On what themes and/or ideas is the preparation to be based?
7 What are the possible developments and progressions?
8 What skill learning may take place?
9 How will the children be (a) stimulated initially and as the work proceeds, (b) organized?
10 Is any integration possible with other subjects?

Short-term preparation indicates the making of lesson notes for a particular lesson, the activity being based on the themes planned in the scheme but very much dependent on what developed in the previous lesson. This is an important point, for it ensures that the teacher is constantly aware of the need to teach *the children*, rather than the activity. The teacher may find it helpful to have some clear organization of lesson notes as indicated below. The comments column should remain empty until after the lesson when, as a result of his keen observation, the teacher should, as soon as possible, complete it with an account of what work developed and how the children reacted and progressed. The detail in this column is the basis of the next lesson preparation, for it indicates which activities need to be progressed and which, having served their purpose, should be discarded. It should be clear from this that no lesson can ever be an exact repetition of the previous one, for this would indicate that the latter completely lacked development of activity and understanding.

LESSON NOTES

Date: Type of Lesson: Age: Time:

Aim: No. in class:

Organization	*Limitations*	*Possible coaching*	*Comments*
INTRODUCTION			
(a) Free Practice			
(b) Introductory Activity			
FLOOR TRAINING			
(a) Whole body			
(b) Legs			
(c) Weight on hands			
CLIMAX	TASKS		
Class working in six groups of six	Diagram showing lay-out of apparatus and group places.	1 2 3 4 5 6	
CONCLUSION			

Chapter 3

The Scope – Laban's Principles

We all have two sides to our nature, a conservative, imitative side, and an adventurous, creative side, and all teachers need to take both into account in all education, including physical education.

It is the *conservative side* of our nature that accounts for our love of rhythm and repetition which results in the mastery of our environment. If we learn from others around us, and imitate them, we feel safe and adequate and capable of dealing with day-to-day happenings. Each repetition – the routine of environment as it is called – is reassuring to this side of us.

In physical education the repetition of known activities satisfies this conservative side of the child's make-up. He has pleasure in repeating a pattern of movement or in playing a known game. It gives confidence to feel sure of what is coming next and to know that he will be adequate.

As against this we all have, in different degrees, an adventurous, assertive, *creative side* that craves for challenges and for opportunities of exploration and self-expression, of improving on a previous performance.

The *scope* of physical education should be such that children are given the confidence and enterprise that comes from the alternating rhythm of repetitive and creative activity. At the least this indicates gymnastics (including apparatus work), games, dance, athletics and swimming; at the most the whole field of physical activity presents an infinite variety.

LABAN'S PRINCIPLES

Common to all aspects of physical education is movement. Rudolf Laban developed an analysis of movement which resulted in the formulation of *movement principles*. Laban related these to dance, drama and industrial movement only, but they have since received

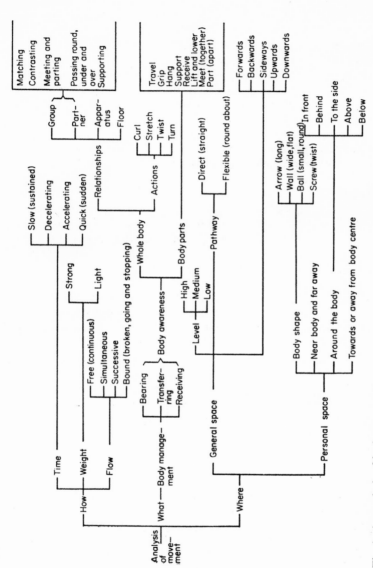

Fig. 1. An analysis of body movement.

a broader application; more successfully in gymnastics, with some reservations with reference to skills.

Movement Principles

The *body* is the instrument of human movement. Thus, if the child is being educated physically, he must acquire an increasing knowledge of the instrument involved. He should become aware of where one body part is and what it does in relation to other parts or to the whole. This learning is termed '*body awareness*'.

Certain *factors* are common to all movement – the factors of *space*, *weight*, *time* and *flow*. These give the means of analysing movement, for all actions are a blending, in various degrees, of these qualities.

Space:

The body occupies its own personal space which reaches from a stationary position as far as the normal extension of any body part in any direction or level. Any movement outside these limits takes the body into the general space which it shares with others. This movement may follow either a direct (straight) or flexible (round-about) path; the body may be moving in a forward, backward or sideways direction; and at a high, medium or low level. The shape of the body in movement is constantly changing between arrow (long and extended), ball (small and rounded), wall (wide) and screw (twisted).

Weight:

In this connection the term does not refer merely to the use of body weight, though with younger children the experience of 'strong' and 'light' is a stage in the development of an appreciation of the true quality of muscular energy and tension. Thus 'strong' becomes 'with tension' and 'light' develops into 'without tension'.

Time:

The performance of any movement uses a quantity of time. For younger children this may be experienced as 'quick' or 'slow', though neither speed nor rhythm is involved in the quality of time, which shows itself properly in the use of a little time, that is with 'sudden-ness', or using much time, that is with 'sustainment'.

Flow:

The flow of movement can be either 'bound' or 'free'. A 'bound flow' action is one which can easily be checked or held, whereas a movement which is difficult to stop suddenly is termed 'free flow'. One effect of altering the emphasis placed on any of these factors can be seen in the use to which we put movement. In this sense movement may be either 'functional' and will predominate in muscular effort (*weight*) and 'bound flow', or it will be 'expressive' with full use being made of accent and phrasing (*weight*) and 'free flow'. Thus, based on the common principles, movement diverges in use:

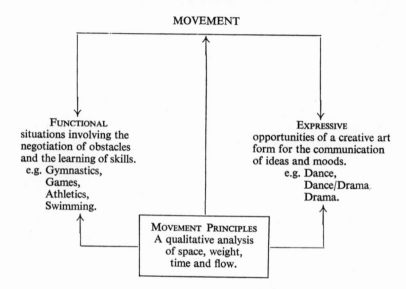

MOVEMENT

FUNCTIONAL
situations involving the
negotiation of obstacles
and the learning of skills.
e.g. Gymnastics,
    Games,
    Athletics,
    Swimming.

EXPRESSIVE
opportunities of a creative art
form for the communication
of ideas and moods.
e.g. Dance,
    Dance/Drama.
    Drama.

MOVEMENT PRINCIPLES
A qualitative analysis
of space, weight,
time and flow.

Chapter 4

The Primary Programme – Development of a
Lesson Plan – Clothing for Physical Activity –
Preparation of the Hall

The physical education of the child is a continuous process and it is
only for convenience that discussion and planning of the primary
and secondary programmes are separated.

THE PRIMARY PROGRAMME

The work in the primary school may be said to be basic to that
planned for the secondary stage. This indicates a concentration of
area for the primary stage with a consequent widening of scope in
the secondary school; a plan which fits in with the increasing
capacity, interests and abilities of the child.

Hence, for the primary school, we aim at a programme which, if
possible, includes:

1 Gymnastics, using as obstacles, small and large apparatus
2 Games training, using appropriate small apparatus
3 Dance
4 Swimming.

It is an easy matter to justify the minimum of a daily physical education lesson at the primary stage. This can be claimed even in schools
where physical education is thought of solely as an antidote to
sedentary work – an opportunity to 'let off steam'. In an enlightened
curriculum the link between motor experience and intellectual
progress is fully appreciated and physical education lessons are seen
as a further valuable means of development. Also to be appreciated
is the possibility of new relationships resulting from meeting other
children and the teacher on different and, to them, highly significant
ground. The teacher's personal refreshment and fitness can be

considered as a further argument in favour of regular, organized physical activity for the class.

The way in which the time is divided may be dependent on the facilities available in the school, and pressure on the school hall will be of special importance. The teacher should be ready to adapt to the weather and the season by taking more of the outdoor type of lesson, thus ensuring that children get the full benefit of sunshine, warmth and fresh air.

The length of lesson should increase as the child moves further up the school. Whereas the 5-year-old needs a proportion of the allocated 30 minutes for changing (a slow business at first but necessary for social training and independence) which may leave only 20 minutes actual working time, the junior child requires the entire half hour for activity, and changing time should be additional. Fortunately the junior is skilful and quick in his preparation, especially with the incentive of exciting and purposeful work ahead.

DEVELOPMENT OF A LESSON PLAN

The principles governing the logical development of a lesson in any subject apply equally to all types of physical education, at least at the primary stage. The class needs first of all to be introduced to the topic or interest of the lesson, the theme is then developed by practising the necessary skill or vocabulary, then application is needed to consolidate what has been learnt. Lastly, the lesson is rounded off so that the children are left with a feeling of satisfaction and security.

In physical education the lesson plan has this basic form:

1 Introduction.
2 Training
3 Climax
4 Conclusion.

The plan is then adapted to the different types of lesson mentioned above. This adaptation will be dealt with in the ensuing chapters.

To get full benefit from the work planned, effort and interest should climb gradually from the opening activity to their peak in the climax. This is important physiologically, for heart and limbs should not have great demands made on them until they have been 'warmed up'. It is important too for safety in dealing with apparatus as warm, relaxed hands and feet are necessary for gripping and balancing. A further point that should be made is that children must be given the opportunity to do suitable and thoughtful work in the training part of the lesson if they are to feel adequate and capable in the climax. Thus, although the greater proportion of the time available (just over half) should be spent on the climax, it is obvious that if this is to be skilful and safe, the previous parts of the lesson cannot, under any circumstances, be omitted.

CLOTHING FOR PHYSICAL ACTIVITY

Another essential consideration for safe and worth-while activity is that the children should wear the minimum of clothing. Indoors, and in warm weather out of doors, younger children need only wear pants, a vest being added for older girls. Feet should be bare whenever possible but, if work is to be done out of doors or if the hall floor is unsuitable, rubber-soled and flexible shoes must be worn. The wearing of socks without shoes, besides being wasteful and extravagant, is a highly dangerous practice as socks slip more easily than shoes or feet. To justify the discarding of extra clothes, the teacher must by his preparation and teaching ensure an active and stimulating lesson.

No jewellery of any kind should be worn during physical education lessons, both because of its unsuitability for the activity and the possibility of accidents.

After a vigorous lesson, the children should be warm if not perspiring. Ideally it should be possible for them to have a quick shower before changing into their ordinary clothes. Where school showers are not available, at least hands should be washed and the teacher should take the opportunity to stress the value to the community and the individual of regular washing and bathing, particularly after warming exercise. The putting on of the extra sweater after the lesson ensures that the body cools slowly, thus preventing chill and the consequent criticism of parents who object to their child stripping for physical education.

The teacher as well should set a workmanlike example by changing into suitable clothing if possible. As a minimum shoes should be changed, and, in the case of a woman teacher, a skirt allowing free movement will ensure safety.

PREPARATION OF THE HALL

As long as the system of providing an all-purpose hall in primary schools persists, it will be necessary to prepare the hall for physical education to ensure that the children can get full benefit from using the maximum of space and to ensure *safety*. Forms and chairs and dining tables, if they must be in the hall, should be stacked neatly and safely against one wall if possible, the wall least likely to be important in considering the arrangement of physical education apparatus. In particular, the piano and stool should be pushed

back against a wall or into a corner, as so often these jut dangerously
into the space. Physical education apparatus, large and small,
should be arranged around the room, accessible from the area
where it will be required for class and group activities. The floor
should be clean and this may involve sweeping and/or swabbing,
especially after the school lunch – it is neither pleasant nor safe to
have pieces of food left lying on a floor which is to be used for some
form of physical activity.

Windows should be *opened* to ensure a supply of fresh, moving air,
adequate for the class coming in for their lesson. Incidentally, this
is a good time to open the windows in the classroom being vacated,
for it ensures a pleasant and fresh atmosphere for the children when
they return after their activity.

Chapter 5

The Primary Programme (continued) – Gymnastics

GYMNASTICS

The name 'gymnastics' no longer has the remedial connotation of 'exercises developing the muscles' but in the present-day approach denotes that aspect of physical education which provides 'the grammar of whole body movement' necessary to negotiate obstacles successfully, skilfully and safely. The body in this context is being used functionally and with agility in a challenging situation.

On first entering school the child finds sufficient challenge in the size and nature of the hall or playground. His physical education commences therefore with adventurous investigation of the new environment. The gymnastics lesson should take place in the hall and the floor will continue to be a most important piece of apparatus as the place where the child tries out new skills and ideas before transferring them to the higher, and therefore more difficult, situations provided by other apparatus.

Exploration

It has been made clear earlier that the young child learns first through exploration and this will be applied to the gymnastic lesson, but for the child's safety some direct teaching must precede this. Such teaching is aimed at *spacing* and *response* and can be quickly developed through the simple action of running. Actually, the child's immediate and natural reaction to the large space in hall or playground will be to run. The teacher can make deliberate use of this fact. While running anywhere the class can be given practice in responding to the word 'stop' and will enjoy this as a game, meanwhile benefiting from the control it helps to develop. As they run, such phrases as 'Run into spaces', 'Try not to bump anybody', 'Find a space', 'Run by yourself' will encourage good use of space. Soft, light feet, if encouraged, will add to safety at speed. All of this will not, of course, be learnt in one lesson – it will be repeated and, in fact, a similar approach can be made in dance and games training.

Such an introduction to the first gymnastic lesson(s) could be followed by free exploration of an assortment of large and small apparatus set out ready and easily pulled into the space by the teacher.

A Note on Apparatus

The children themselves will gradually be trained to lift, carry and erect their own apparatus, but meanwhile the teacher should organize this with the help of auxiliaries and bigger children. Much to be deplored is an increasing tendency in primary schools to have the apparatus erected by the caretaker for use by every class on only one day in the week. Such a system has three main faults:

1 It imposes the same set pattern of apparatus situations on all classes in the school, thus denying and inhibiting progression based on the individual needs of the children's ages and stages. This in fact produces boredom for the older children.

2 The children miss the worth-while physical and social satisfaction of moving their own apparatus.

3 There is lack of body training on the floor with the immediate carry-over to the apparatus challenge. Children of all ages need for safety reasons the previous warming and limbering of the body, before climbing on to apparatus, but younger children especially need the immediate application of what the body can do, their mental and physical memory being, as yet, short-lived.

Some direct teaching and careful supervision are, of course, necessary to ensure that such carrying and erecting of apparatus can be achieved safely and successfully by younger children. If the teacher has the patience and ability to progress and develop such learning, the results are educationally sound. At a time when choice of apparatus is wide, and widening, it should be possible to select sections appropriate to the different ages and increasing size and skill of the children concerned. Indeed, many primary schools base their choice of apparatus on the grounds of 'what the children can lift, carry and erect (with training and supervision) is suitable for their use'.

The child has begun to learn to use space and to manage his body and this *body management* continues to be the basis of primary school gymnastics.

Developing the Activity

Important though the exploratory stage is in gymnastics, it must be gradually replaced by something more purposeful. This is essential to fit in with the developing nature of the child but also in order that the 'playlike' activities mentioned in Chapter 2 may give way to a working atmosphere. The change is brought about by the increasing use of *tasks*, i.e. challenges in more specific terms.

Tasks impose certain limitations on the activity the children will perform, these limitations being wide at first and gradually narrowing as the children become more experienced in movement and able to perform more difficult and demanding work.

Tasks are set:

1 To make the child think as well as use his physical faculties
2 To encourage each child to work within this own capacity and at his own rate
3 To stimulate each child's inventiveness and purpose
4 To widen the child's movement experience by finding different ways of solving the problem
5 To ensure that a limited number of favourite activities are not repeated indefinitely by individual children
6 To progress the child's movement ability by limiting his choice.

Observation and Analysis

Observation and analysis of individual efforts were referred to in Chapter 2 as fundamental teaching technique in the present-day approach. They depend on the teacher asking himself certain questions. The first question to ask in looking at movement is WHAT is the body doing? This is more easily answered if the teacher concentrates on the way in which the children handle the weight of the body. In the young child the answer is usually to be found in terms of *locomotion* (i.e. propelling and transferring his body weight), for he is rarely static. But through practice, and as he matures, he becomes more able to work in terms of *receiving* and *bearing* his weight. The following table provides starting and developing points for such learning.

MANAGING THE BODY
(WHAT is the body doing?)

Propelling and trans-ferring body weight	Receiving body weight	Bearing body weight
Running	Arriving	Balancing
Walking	Landing	Hanging
Skipping	Lowering	Holding
Jumping	Rolling	Rocking
Climbing		Swinging
Rolling		
Sliding		
Spinning		

It will be noticed that the terms used refer to the 'whole body' and, as the young child's ability lies in big body movement, this is appropriate. Education, however, implies progress, and in this instance progress must lie in a growing *body awareness*, i.e. a knowledge of where parts of the body are and what they are doing in relation to other parts and to the whole. Thus we give the child increasing opportunities to experience the movements of which his whole body is capable: *curling, stretching, twisting,* and *turning* – and the actions of parts: *travelling, gripping, supporting, hanging, receiving, lifting, meeting, parting.* We begin this experience by giving simple, clearly understood tasks which use aspects of body management (WHAT?) such as in what ways can the body be handled on feet, hands and feet, and then other body parts. While the children are experiencing and feeling the actions the teacher can gradually bring out the simple terms to describe them (running, jumping, rolling).

He then goes on to ask himself the next two questions about movement, HOW? and WHERE?, and simple terminology can gradually be brought out to describe it, e.g. quick, slow, light, high, low, smooth, jerky, curled, twisted, stretched. In this way each child will begin to build up a *movement vocabulary*.

It must be stressed that although verbalizing his physical experience is important to the child's understanding of movement, it is not the most important aspect of the lesson – *activity* is the first aim and must not give way to discussion.

Chapter 6

The Primary Programme (continued) –
The Gymnastic Lesson Plan (Stages I and II)

While each child works as an individual the teacher cannot anticipate exactly how the work in a lesson will develop. At the same time he needs to have a plan of activities to be initiated. The lesson plan suggested in Chapter 4 is adapted for gymnastics thus:

STAGE I: EXPLORATORY

1 Introduction

Suggestions to be progressed over a number of lessons:

(I) Running in the space avoiding everybody else. Give practice in stopping quite still in a space. Coach 'Try not to bump anybody', 'Run by yourself', 'Run into the spaces'.

(II) Running softly, changing to stamping the feet heavily into the floor, repeat running softly. Use the contrasting movement to emphasize running with soft feet.

(III) Which part of you is touching the floor? Show another way of moving about with your feet touching the floor – develop one or more of the answers (they will probably include walking, jumping, skipping, etc.).

(IV) Find another part to help your feet to move about the floor. The answer will most probably be hands (the answer should be in action) – encourage all to try this way so that hands and feet run, walk (crawl), jump, etc., to link with the exploratory use of them on apparatus later in the lesson.

(V) Develop the use of other body parts to help the feet, or take the place of feet, in moving about the floor, e.g. knees and bottom can step, bottom and back can jump, front and back can slide and spin, etc.

Continue to stress spacing and response to the teacher's word. (See page 30.)

2 Free Exploration on Assembled Apparatus

The teacher provides situations with the apparatus which will give opportunities for climbing, sliding, swinging, jumping off, staying on, walking, crawling, hanging, rolling, etc.

Apart from asking them to find out what they can do on the apparatus he should not, at this stage, suggest activities or encourage the children to attempt anything they have not thought of for themselves. He should move about showing interest in what is being attempted, observing the abilities and inventiveness of individuals and continuing to encourage spacing as on the floor. Further training in response can be given, the children stopping quite still on the apparatus at the teacher's word and then climbing down by the shortest route – this should not involve *speed*!

3 Conclusion

Relaxed, calming movement or position on the floor, e.g. curl up small in a space, stand up tall.

It will depend on the progress made by the class how soon the teacher goes on from the exploratory stage. He may think they have enough confidence and ability to move gradually into Stage II when:

(a) All children are joining in freely
(b) They are using the space well
(c) They are responding quickly to the teacher's word
(d) Most of them are moving freely about the apparatus
(e) A number of children are gripping the apparatus with various body parts (hands, feet, elbows, knees)
(f) Some of the class are sometimes stopping quite still on some parts of the apparatus
(g) The majority are finding places to climb up
(h) They are finding places to slide down as well as jump down.

STAGE II

1 Introduction

(a) *Free Practice*

This part of the lesson begins in the classroom or cloakroom, wherever the children change, by the teacher giving a challenge to be started as soon as they enter the hall and find a space. Instructions should be simple and brief so that the children can retain them and commence work at once without uncertainty. The work suggested should be familiar so that they can get on with it individually without the teacher's presence and help, as he is bringing up the rear and may even need a moment to check that apparatus has been put out ready exactly as planned. This known quality of the free practice may come about because the teacher has chosen a favourite activity such as jumping, which always presents children with challenge and interest. It may, alternatively, be something the class tried in the previous lesson which gripped their interest and which they will therefore wish to practise immediately.

The advantages of having the children immediately active on entering the hall are obvious but nonetheless important to state:

(i) Economy of time, as the lesson is already too short, especially if much has been spent (necessarily) in changing.

(ii) Getting the lesson off to a good start gives the keynote of enjoyment and activity.

(iii) Gripping the class with purposeful activity within the scope of all the children prevents any lack of discipline from the outset and establishes concentration.

(iv) Preliminary limbering and warming of the body is useful, physically and physiologically, and leads each child at his own pace into the more vigorous activity to follow.

(b) *Introductory Activity*

The work started in the introductory activity in Stage I should be developed, the teacher challenging the children by simply worded tasks to move freely about the whole floor space.

WHAT? From the answers given, words describing the actions will emerge, thus involving the children in observing and thinking. Also, as already mentioned, different movement qualities will be experienced and described in simple words and phrases such as:

WHERE? *Space:*

Body shape – wide, thin, tall, curled, twisted, stretched, screwed, big, small, using a little space, using a lot of space.

Level of movement – high, medium, low, near the floor, nearest the ceiling, high up, away from the floor, on the floor, in the air, far from the floor.

Relationship of parts – hands near to feet, hands far from feet, feet apart, feet together, hands apart, hands near.

Direction of movement – forward, backward, sideways, turning.

Pathway of movement – straight, curly, zigzag, curved, round about, square, figure of eight.

Relationship with the hall – facing the floor, facing the ceiling.

HOW?   *Weight:*

Tension - light, heavy.

Energy – gentle, strong.
Sound – soft, quiet, loud.

HOW?   *Time:*

Rhythm – quick, sudden, slow, lingering.
Speed – slowly, slower, gradually, fast, faster.

HOW?   *Flow:*

Sensation – jerky, careful, smooth.
Balance – still, stopping, going, flying.

Many of the words and phrases can be seen to occur in contrasting pairs and further evidence of this comes out in the suggestions made throughout this chapter. This 'teaching by contrast' helps the child to appreciate the quality of movement concerned.

Suggestions for tasks developing locomotion (travelling, i.e. 'moving about the space') started in the Exploratory Stage:

(i) Run anywhere and when you see a space jump as high as you can in it.

(ii) Move about the space taking small steps. Change to taking long steps. (Bring out the change in body level.) Can you find another way of moving low down near the floor with only feet touching? (Develop bouncing and stepping from the children's answers.) Now find a way which takes you up towards the ceiling with feet touching the floor.

(iii) Move about the floor on your heels (toes, side of foot, etc.). Now try one foot (stress frequent changes to the other foot as hopping is tiring). Find a way of moving about with your feet close together, now far apart.

(iv) Travel about the space using feet and making a curly pattern. Change to a straight line pattern. Step a straight line pattern. Run in a zigzag. (This can be developed up into the junior school where the children still enjoy stepping, galloping and jumping: letters, figures, names, circles, figures of eight, etc.)

(v) Move on hands and feet quickly. Coach head up always when weight is over hands until the children have learnt how to over-balance safely. (In response to the task the children will probably go forward – pick out someone going backward or sideways and help them to identify the different direction and then all try it.)

(vi) Travel on hands and feet slowly. (This may result in some children using a lot of space. Help the class to become aware of this and all try it – then all try 'Travel on hands and feet using a little space'.)

(vii) Move about with hands and feet on the floor close to each other. Now far apart. (Develop stepping with hands then feet, and 'pouncing' on to hands and jumping feet up to them.)

(viii) Move on hands and feet with seat nearest the ceiling. Which part is facing the floor? Try with back facing the floor. Which part is nearest the ceiling now? (Having experienced the turn over they can develop this as a way of travelling, i.e. turning continuously sideways on hands and feet. Check spacing!)

(ix) Try travelling about the space on two hands and one foot, then one hand and two feet. (Bring in different directions.)

(x) Walk about the space on another part, not feet. (The children may use knees, seat.) Find another way of moving on your seat. (Some children will jump.) Let your heels or hands help your seat.

(xi) Move backwards on your seat with your hands helping.

(xii) Find a way of moving on your front with hands helping. Try going backwards as well as forwards. Can you find another direction?

(xiii) Curl up and move softly along the floor. (The children will probably roll without any further suggestion.) Try rolling in a different direction.

(xiv) Stretch out and find a way to move about the space. Change direction.

2 Floor Training

This part of the lesson is especially concerned with body management in *transferring, bearing* and *receiving* of body weight, and is therefore absolutely essential to safety and skill on the apparatus. For this reason all three parts should be included in each lesson. If shortage of time makes three separate activities impossible some combination is possible (e.g. weight on hands can involve the legs in a jump or running round the hands) or compensation can be made in a subsequent lesson.

(a) *Work for the Whole Body*

Basic to the use of the whole body in transferring and receiving weight is the ability to bear its weight on parts, including hands and feet. The balance of the body in bearing weight is affected by its shape, so these two things are linked.

Suggested tasks:

(i) Curl up small with feet touching the floor. Find a way of stretching out with feet touching the floor.

(ii) Find another part of you to curl up on. (Develop knees, shins, back, shoulders, side, hands.) Try stretching out on that part. Go on finding all the parts of the body you can curl up on and try stretching out on them too.

(iii) Move about with your weight on a part and your body curled (stretched).

(iv) Balance on a part and make a different body shape (wide, twisted, one-sided). Try these shapes on other parts of the body.

(v) Curl up with weight on a body part – *rock* there. Encourage a vigorous rocking until body balance is lost and weight is naturally transferred to an adjacent part of the body.

(vi) Stretch out with your weight on a part of your body and rock. Rock until balance is lost and move to an adjacent body part.
(*Note:* The *rocking* action on the floor is not only good preparation for rolling but it gives the child ample experience of being 'off balance' which is invaluable when he accidentally meets such a situation in his experiments on the apparatus. When this occurs, his body automatically draws on past experience and recovers balance by moving on to an adjacent part.)

(vii) Curl up on a part and roll softly. Roll quickly, roll slowly.

(viii) Start with a stretch with the body resting on any part, roll and stand up.

(ix) Travel curled up with a roll and stand up.

(x) Roll curled up (stretched out) and use hands to jump up.
(*Note:* This is a most important stage as it is probably the child's first deliberate attempt to transfer from one body part to a non-adjacent part (i.e. not next to each other, e.g. from seat to hands to feet.)

(xi) Roll curled up (stretched out) and jump up without hands.

(xii) Standing, find body parts to *put* down on to the floor. Curl up there. Roll and jump up.

(xiii) Walk, *put* a body part down and roll curled up (stretched out) and jump up. Increase from a slow to a quick walk, to a run, before putting the body part down.
(*Note:* Emphasize at first the careful putting down of a part.)

(b) *Work for the Legs*

The legs have two important functions in connection with managing the body weight:

1 Propulsion (take off)
2 Landings

Both must be catered for: propulsion for flight and adventurous work on the apparatus, and landings to ensure safety in coming off heights.

Suggested tasks:

(i) Jump in a space. Notice that someone jumps on one foot (hopping) – all try it – someone else from foot to foot, (leaping) – all try it – someone else bounces on two feet – all try it. Encourage jumping in all ways, sometimes using one foot then the other, one foot all the time, two feet then one, one foot then two, two feet all the time, two feet near together, two feet apart.

(*Note:* This experience at a very simple level of the *five basic jumps* is essential to the development of propulsion (spring) for *flight* in apparatus work but, like rocking (see Whole Body), it also develops a built-in safety factor – the child builds up experience in going off-balance and recovering balance while moving from one foot to the same, or to the other, or to two feet on the floor. When such a situation arises unexpectedly in working with apparatus he responds with the proper adjustment of weight through his use of feet.)

(ii) Jump on two feet springing high on each jump (resilience for take off, or for alighting in preparation for going on).

(iii) Jump on two feet landing deeply, tucking the tail under and sitting down on heels. Land softly.

(iv) Run and jump into a space landing deeply and softly.

(v) Run and jump into a space springing off and running on repeating the jump.

(vi) Leap in all the spaces.

(vii) Run and leap and land deeply on two feet.

(viii) Run and jump into a curled shape.

(ix) Run and jump into a stretched shape.

(x) Run and jump into a wide shape.

(xi) Run and jump landing deeply with a turn.

(xii) Run and jump into a twisted shape. Repeat twisting to the other side.

(c) *Weight on Hands*

This part of the floor training is essential to strengthen the shoulder, arm and back muscles so that the children, when using the apparatus, can lift or jump the hips and legs over with weight supported on hands (flat or gripping). The strengthening effect is also seen in climbing, hanging and swinging.

Suggested tasks:

(i) Hands firmly on floor in front (check hands pointing forward, fingers close, shoulder distance apart to get the best support). Head up! The children may have already tried some of the ways of moving about the room on hands and feet or two hands and one foot or one hand and two feet (see Introductory Activity Suggestions). Remind them of some of these. Stop in a space and lift one foot high – Head up! – as soon as one foot is lifted, the body will experience the pushing forward of weight over shoulders and hands. Try the other foot.

(ii) Hands on floor – Head up! – run feet round the hands, sometimes near to them and sometimes far away.

(iii) Hands on floor – Head up! – kick one leg up and then the other. Come down softly with feet near to hands. Try again and see if you can do more than one kick before coming down softly – keep the head up while kicking.

(iv) Hands on floor – Head up! – jump both legs up off the floor and bring them down together at the side. Repeat to the other side (this produces an experience of landing from an off-balance position which will be useful in managing the body when this happens unexpectedly).

(iii) and (iv) can be developed so that the two feet leave the floor separately or together and land separately or together. Stress the soft landing so as to prevent a jarring impact, besides developing control in the muscles of hips, legs and feet.

3 Climax

This part of the lesson should take roughly half, or slightly more than half, of the teaching time available: e.g. in 20 minutes teaching time 10 to 12 minutes should be left for working with and on apparatus, so that the children have time to work with application.

Although the children have had a number of lessons on the large apparatus (Stage I – Exploratory) it is a good idea when commencing Stage II to leave this and begin making use of small apparatus on a *class activity method* for the following reasons:

(a) The handling of small apparatus is more within the grasp (hand grasp) of the younger children and therefore can provide basic and progressive training in fetching, carrying and arranging it in spaces. The teacher can insist on careful handling and putting down *quietly* in the spaces.

(b) The supply is usually greater and therefore ensures enough for everybody so there is no waiting for turns and limiting of experience.

(c) Small apparatus lacks the height of the large and therefore provides a safe and confidence-giving situation for developing new knowledge about body management (additional to what the child has discovered for himself by exploration).

(d) Small apparatus can give scope, interest and purpose to the child's work, and this will be important when he meets it later on, supplementing the supply of large apparatus in group work.

(e) The use of small apparatus stresses the need for space in using apparatus of any kind and this draws attention to the important fact that any piece of apparatus can be approached from many angles.

(f) The class activity method ensures that the children know the task and it develops the link for them between work on the floor and work with the apparatus.

Small Apparatus

This should include hoops (suitable to the size of the children), individual ropes, individual mats, canes, skittles.

Note: Apparatus such as bats, balls and bean bags is not included here because the object of these lessons is to develop skilled body movement, whereas skills such as throwing, catching, striking a ball and skipping in a rope will be developed in the games training lesson out of doors.

Suggestions for class activity tasks with small apparatus:

Note: It should be possible to take two or three Class Activities consecutively in a lesson, maybe with a change of apparatus to give variety and interest.

(i) Each child with a hoop. Run round your hoop – changes of direction. Find other ways of going round with feet. Use other body parts with feet – hands, knees, bottom, etc. – without feet.

Go across your hoop using feet, hands and feet, etc.

Go in and out of your hoop on one foot, two feet, hands and feet – other body parts.

Hold your hoop in one hand and get through it. Which part of your body went through first? Let another part lead you. Which direction is the body moving in? Try another direction. Hold the hoop with the other hand.

Support hoop between or across chairs – stepping, jumping, crawling, sliding, rolling, curling, stretching and twisting through will develop. Different parts of the body leading.

(ii) Each child with a rope lays it along the floor in a line.

Find ways of moving around (along); using feet, hands and feet, other body parts.

Go across the rope using feet, hands and feet, other body parts.

Move from side to side of the rope; using feet, hands and feet, other body parts.

Place the rope in a curly or wavy pattern – jump in and out of the spaces. Alter the pattern to round, square, etc., and find ways of getting round, across, etc.

(iii) Each child with a small mat – develop ways of going around, across, along, etc.; using feet, hands and feet, other body parts; by stepping, jumping, rolling, sliding, spinning.

(iv) Canes supported on skittles or chairs.

Develop ways of getting over and under, round, in and out; using feet, hands and feet, other body parts; by stepping, crawling, jumping, rolling, sliding, spinning, curling, twisting, stretching.

(v) Boxes, drama apparatus, dinner forms (if tested for safety), can gradually be added and the same sort of things developed in terms of pathway words (about, along, around, through, across, over, etc.); and actions (run, step, jump, slide, spin, etc.); and body parts to be used (feet, hands and feet, other body parts).

From this point the small apparatus may:

1 Have to be used in combination to provide challenging situations *if there is no large apparatus available in the school* (see Fig. 2).

2 Be used to supplement the large apparatus *if there is not a sufficient supply of large apparatus to cater for all the children in a class* (see Fig. 3).

3 Be limited in its use to the floor training where it can continue to help the children to develop body management for use on the large apparatus *if there is a sufficient supply of large apparatus to cater for all the children in a class* (see Fig. 4).

Use of Agility and Climbing Apparatus

The work done with small apparatus will have accustomed the children to working with purpose, finding as many ways as possible within the limitations of the task set by the teacher. This is a progression on the exploratory work they did at first on the large apparatus.

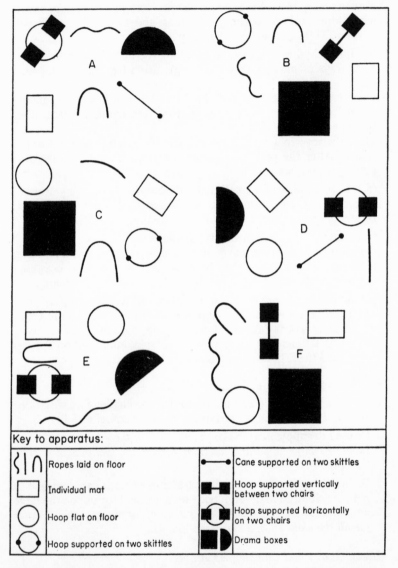

Key to apparatus:

〈│∩	Ropes laid on floor	●━━●	Cane supported on two skittles
▭	Individual mat	◼━◼	Hoop supported vertically between two chairs
◯	Hoop flat on floor	◼◉◼	Hoop supported horizontally on two chairs
◉	Hoop supported on two skittles	◼◖	Drama boxes

Fig. 2. An arrangement of small apparatus to develop work in six groups.

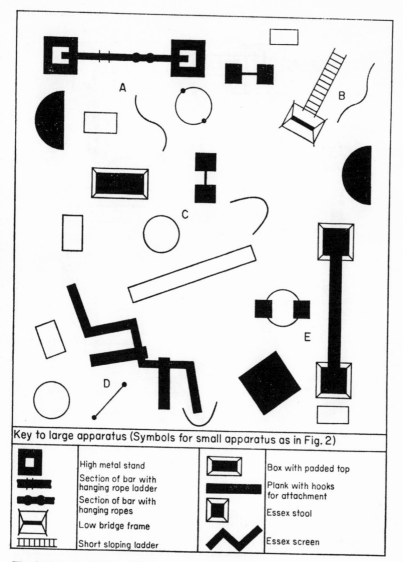

Key to large apparatus (Symbols for small apparatus as in Fig. 2)

High metal stand		Box with padded top
Section of bar with hanging rope ladder		Plank with hooks for attachment
Section of bar with hanging ropes		Essex stool
Low bridge frame		Essex screen
Short sloping ladder		

Fig. 3. An arrangement of large apparatus, supplemented by small, to develop work in five groups.

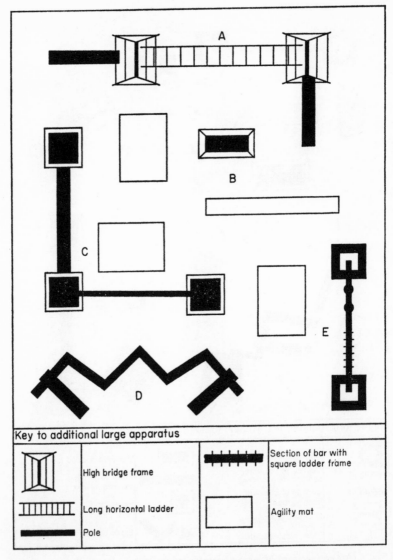

Fig. 4. An arrangement of large apparatus to develop work in five groups.

Therefore, when they again begin to work on the large apparatus their attitude will be different – they will be ready to work to a task of the type which establishes their relationship with the apparatus, i.e. an *action task* where the apparatus sets the problem:

e.g. 'Move *along* the plank'.

The word 'along' defines the relationship.

Many L.E.A.s have their own design of agility and climbing apparatus. The *Essex Agility Apparatus* was introduced in the first place for primary school children and can be used in any hall or level playground or field. It is of wood and consists of:

(a) Two pairs of stools, 2 feet 9 inches and 2 feet 3 inches high and with five and four rungs respectively;
(b) One six-fold screen 2 feet 6 inches in height;
(c) Six 7-foot planks with hinged hooks both ends;
(d) Two 7-foot poles with hooked ends.

The apparatus can be easily carried and adjusted by the children. The screen is taken apart and moved in six sections.

The *stools* allow climbing on and off, jumping off, crawling through, etc. They are also used to support the planks and poles steadily at convenient heights for running up and down and for sliding and jumping.

The *screen* is used for balancing along the top and for climbing through and over or for weaving in and out, as well as turning over the horizontal bars.

The *planks* are used for running, crawling, sliding and jumping up and down and also for lying, pulling up or down by the hands. If inclined at an angle, the under surface presents opportunities for hanging by hands and feet.

The *poles* allow for hanging and travelling along supported by hands, feet and knees and for hanging and turning over.

The apparatus is relatively cheap and can be stored in a space 7 feet by 2 feet 6 inches. It is designed for primary children; to be strong enough for the older and heavier performers it would have to be heavier and would not be as readily portable as it is now.

Other firms produce types of apparatus which, because of the greater height possible by using metal in combination with wood, give the children opportunities for climbing.

The *Olympic Gymnastic* consists of trestle trees, poles, stools, frames and ladders.

Carco combines metal, wood and padded surfaces in arrangements of frames, hanging ropes, bars, benches, balancing beams, ladders. This type of apparatus requires fixing devices to be inserted in the walls of the hall and is not therefore mobile.

On the other hand, some types may be used in and out of doors; for instance *Croxdale, Whittle, Wicksteeds, Bristol* and *Hunt* climbing apparatus, all of which mainly comprise tubular steel frames, bars, ladders, rope nets and trestles.

DEVELOPMENT OF APPARATUS WORK

Based on arrangements 1, 2 and 3. (Figs 2, 3 and 4.)

Work with apparatus in the climax of the lesson may be developed as follows, each phase succeeding the last according to the progress made by the particular class in terms of:

    (a) increased body management;

    (b) movement vocabulary, especially of pathway words, body parts;

    (c) spacing and response;

    (d) readiness to work and share together in a group (relate to the classroom).

Phase 1

Class Activity. Children moving freely about the apparatus (with regard for overcrowding and safety). The use of the term class activity implies that the children will complete two or three tasks given consecutively.

Suggested tasks:

(i) Get over as many pieces of apparatus as possible.

(ii) See how many pieces of apparatus you can get under.

(iii) Find out how many pieces of apparatus you can go round.

(iv) How many pieces of apparatus can you climb on to? Find a way of getting down. Remember to use your feet softly as you come down.

(v) Find different places on the apparatus where you can hang (swing, travel) with hands (hands and feet).

Phase II

Class Activity. Children remain at a place of their choice (with due regard for overcrowding and safety) and carry out a task set by the teacher. He may suggest they move to a different place for the next task, so accustoming them to the idea of moving on, in preparation for this procedure in group work.

Suggested tasks:

(i) Find different ways of getting on (off, over, round, through) your apparatus. Choose one that you like and repeat it.

(ii) Move about your apparatus using hands and feet only, feet only.

(iii) Can you stay still on your apparatus on another body part, not hands and feet? Curl up on that part. Can you stretch out on that part? Move along the top of your apparatus on that part. Find another part to be still on and then move along the top of your apparatus on it.

(iv) Can you get under your apparatus? See if you can hang underneath your apparatus. Try moving along on the underneath side of your apparatus.

(v) Travel about your apparatus in as many different ways as possible using your hands and any other part of your body except your feet.

Phase III

Group work. When the children are ready for it they are arranged in small groups, of not more than six and preferably less, each with a section of apparatus.

(a) At first the teacher may leave them to work freely on their section in order to accustom them to sharing the apparatus, working together, taking turns and not interfering with each other's work.

(b) The next part of the progression may be to give them a route to follow, thus providing an opportunity to train the group to start at different places on the apparatus rather than form a queue, e.g.

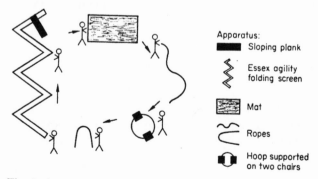

Apparatus:

◼ Sloping plank

⌇ Essex agility folding screen

▦ Mat

∽ Ropes

◖◗ Hoop supported on two chairs

Fig. 5. An arrangement of apparatus to form a route for group work.

(c) The teacher now sets a task – either one task for all sections or a different task for each section. In the latter case, and if the children can read the words to be used, it can help the teacher if he provides each group with a work card, thus saving the time and tedium of going round to each group whilst the others wait to start. The children can refer to the work card as they work, thus ensuring that they keep to the task.

By this time the monitor system will be operating in the classroom and may be applied here so that the group leader can organize the group to start where the work card indicates.

Suggested tasks:

At this stage the children should be ready to do *action tasks* – that is, tasks describing the pathway to be taken in relation to the apparatus and the gaps between the apparatus, and the body parts to be used.

(i) Get on to the stool using hands and feet and travel along the plank on feet only.

(ii) Go across the mat using many body parts and finish with a jump on the floor at the end.

(iii) Get over the cane taking your weight on your hands and feet.

(iv) Come down the plank on a body part, not hands or feet, and roll softly on the floor before standing up.

(v) Get along the underneath side of the ladder using hands and feet. Drop off softly at the end.

(vi) Travel over the mat on your front (or on your bottom).

4 Conclusion

As part of the instruction to put away apparatus the children should be told '. . . and find a space and . . . in it'. This ensures they do not loiter over the job and that they know what to do next, thus preserving the pace and continuity of the lesson. (The same technique can be applied elsewhere in the lesson.)

The purpose of the conclusion is to:

(a) Draw the children together again as a class after their group experience.

(b) Calm and relax them physically and mentally before going along the corridors to the classroom for their next activity.

(c) Leave them with a feeling of poise to take away from the lesson.

Suggested tasks:

(i) Curl up small on your front. Make a very wide shape on your back. Repeat.

(ii) Curl up on your side. Make a strong backward (banana) stretch on your other side. Repeat.

(iii) Crouch down low. Reach up as near the ceiling as possible.

(iv) Curl up small on your back. Stand up tall.

Notes

1 The lists of suggestions made in connection with the lesson plan are not exhaustive but merely indicative of the sorts of things the children should be doing. As the teacher sees the results and appreciates the kind of learning taking place his own understanding will make him better able to word his own tasks specially for the children he is teaching.

2 The work suggested in this chapter has not been arranged in lessons but progression has been made apparent in dealing with the various parts of the lesson plan. It should be evident that the tasks set for apparatus are based on what the children have learnt in the earlier parts of the lesson (as well as on experience in previous lessons) – the child himself should appreciate this linking of his experience.

Chapter 7

The Primary Programme (continued) –
The Climax of the Gymnastic Lesson – Group
Practices – Organization of Apparatus – Group
Leaders – Safety

THE CLIMAX OF THE GYMNASTIC LESSON

The child's interest in the gymnastic lesson builds up towards its peak in the climax where he looks forward to working with apparatus. It is important that his ability and skill should build up towards this point too. As already explained, the first half of the lesson, the training sections, cannot be omitted. Equally important is the inclusion of the work with apparatus. By good timing, and because of his awareness of the children's needs and interests, the teacher will always ensure this balance of activity. Thus in every lesson the children will have the satisfaction of trying out their new-found, or further-developed, body skill on the challenging apparatus situations planned and organized by the teacher.

GROUP PRACTICES

The development of work with apparatus, from the exploratory stage and by means of the class activity method towards the operation of group practices, has been dealt with in the previous chapter.

The advantages of working this way, in units smaller than the class, are that in groups:

1 The children get more turns in the time available.
2 They get the variety of a number of situations.
3 They take turns, group by group, at using apparatus which is limited in quantity, e.g. forms, Essex screen, climbing frame.
4 They get the social training of working together in a smaller, more closely-knit unit.

5 The situation provides an opportunity for some to experience leading and for others to subject themselves to being led.

Note: While one value of the group system is that the children should learn to co-operate readily and to take responsibility, such moral values are not automatically attained. They depend on the teacher's own personality and attitudes, as shown in his teaching and relationships with the children.

ORGANIZATION OF APPARATUS

The use of apparatus raises special problems to do with organizing the distribution and collection of the smaller kinds and the moving and fixing of larger and heavier climbing and gymnastic types.

The teacher must plan ahead and train the children to help in the organization and placing of both kinds of apparatus. There is no time in a short lesson for the teacher to transport the bulk of the apparatus himself, apart from the fact that by doing so he denies the children valuable experience (see Chapter 5). Right from the start of the primary school, in the reception class, children are encouraged to be helpful and self-sufficient and to share in the organization and clearing away of activities. It is proper that this should also apply to physical education lessons and so the children are trained to carry and assemble both small and large apparatus. The *small apparatus* – balls, ropes, hoops, etc. – must be easily moved to the hall or yard in baskets, boxes, or on trolleys, then clearly sorted out and made readily available around the space. The spreading out of the apparatus in this way prevents delay and by dispersing the children also prevents danger, whereas converging on a pile of hoops for instance, especially in a corner, may cause an accident. Training should include the safe way to carry a cane (pointing down with hand near the top), the quiet placing down of a hoop (no kicking of the hoop into another space), safe placing of apparatus in a space (not too near others, nor too close to radiators or to school furniture, such as the piano).

The *large apparatus* should also be organized round the room, in spaces, bordering on the areas in which it will be used later in the lesson. As far as possible this should make it unnecessary for the children to have to carry any large piece of apparatus for long distances – they should only be required to lift it *into* the space. However, as already pointed out in Chapter 5, if the class cannot do the actual manhandling of the apparatus easily, they are not ready to use it.

When planning the apparatus work for the lesson the teacher will obviate too much carrying by organizing the activities to fit in with the placing of the fixed apparatus and the usual storage points of the heavier portable pieces, e.g. work on a box could be arranged in the space nearest to the storage alcove, whereas forms can fairly easily be carried to a space further away across the hall.

Rules should be made to ensure quick and efficient, *but safe*, movement and erection of apparatus:
1 No running with apparatus.
2 Watch out for other people and look for spaces when carrying apparatus.
3 Two people to a form (or four if the forms are heavy and the children small), four people to a large mat, etc.
4 Mats and small apparatus to be placed in position last, to allow free floor space for those carrying large apparatus.
5 No one to get on the apparatus until the teacher has checked bolts, clips, etc.
6 Absolute quiet while moving and placing apparatus – the teacher can make this less of a rigid discipline by praising the resultant efficiency.

On the group system the class is divided into a number of equal-sized groups – six is a convenient number to have in a group, for it is small enough to ensure adequate turns on the apparatus, big enough to foster group feeling and it splits easily into twos or threes for partner work or games practices (if the same groups operate in games training lessons). The same personnel is kept over a length of time and the group identity may be defined by a name, a colour or a leader.

GROUP LEADERS

At first, in the infant school, the leaders do not do much beyond helping the teacher to collect and carry the apparatus and being 'leaders', i.e. giving their name to the group, e.g. 'John's group'. From this time on, leaders will take more responsibility for fetching the correct amount and type of apparatus themselves and may begin to see that the group members work in turns. It is important that, as far as possible, all children should have a turn at being the leader, and the teacher may need to help unobtrusively those who are least fitted for, but most in need of, the experience. Leadership should last for a sufficiently long time to let each leader gain in competence and show his worth, but not so long as to deny some a turn.

The same basic group situations are retained over a series of lessons so that new work is introduced and progresses gradually. The children start at an activity and have a long enough turn to allow each one to experiment, then select, and repeat, the most satisfying and effective solution to the task set. At the teacher's word to stop the children should get down from the apparatus, the nearest way, and stand quietly and tidily ready to move on to the next place – the teacher will have already given clear directions about the route. Another move may take place within the time available, i.e. each group having a turn at three activities. When group work comes round next lesson the teacher should know where the groups finished and go on from there so that all children have a turn with the various pieces of apparatus.

The chief weaknesses that occur in group practices are:

(i) The activities do not balance up in interest because of a paucity of equally challenging apparatus. Thus effort flags in the less demanding situations; (this can be covered to a certain extent by previous training in exploring the interest and challenge of small apparatus described in Chapter 6 *and* by the teacher's appreciation and encouragement).

(ii) Lack of scope in the use of the situations provided because the apparatus is not sufficiently well-spaced-out.

(iii) Failure on the teacher's part to train the children to approach the apparatus from many angles and not just the obvious one.

(iv) Poor timing, resulting in the children being kept at each activity for too long or too short a time, the latter especially leaving the children dissatisfied and frustrated.

SAFETY

It is essential at all times that the teacher should be concerned for the children's safety.

Safety on apparatus is ensured by the teacher:

1 Training the children in the use of floor space and then encouraging them to apply this to work on apparatus.
2 Insisting on correct dress (see page 28); discarding items such as skirts, petticoats, tight jeans, etc. which can hamper free and safe movement; correct footwear or, better still, bare feet.
3 Training the children to respond immediately to his word.
4 Developing body management, especially in reception of weight (landings and rolls) and bearing weight on parts of the body.
5 Training particularly the bearing of weight on hands, in order to accustom the child to supporting the body with strong arm and shoulder muscles.
6 Giving experience in gripping the apparatus with hands, feet, knees, elbows, etc.
7 Training the children to move, carry and erect apparatus properly.

8 Providing apparatus situations and challenges suited to the class's ability and experience.

The teacher will, of course, show appreciation of effort and give encouragement to the children, but he should be careful not to urge them beyond their capacity. At the infant stage (5 to 7) it has been found that, when left to work and progress at their own pace, children choose activities within their individual ability. With juniors, however, the teacher must be prepared for over-adventurousness, for they are becoming increasingly motivated by the competitive spirit. They are challenged and dared by the activities and comments of others, by the urge to show off, to copy or to be praised by the teacher. The latter must temper his encouragement to the adventurous elements in the class, while of course paying due attention to basic training.

Chapter 8

The Primary Programme (continued) – Progression in Gymnastics further up the Primary School

The work developed in Chapter 6 was based on body management and body awareness. The tasks suggested under the lesson headings were aimed at developing the child's natural ability to travel on body parts in terms of pathway, and at promoting his skill in bearing and receiving weight on various body surfaces. At the same time he has been helped to identify (name) the actions he and others selected for travelling and to show *some* awareness of how (quality) and where (space) these actions were performed.

This is clearly shown in the analysis of movement (Fig. 1) where the basic work to be done is shown along the middle of the diagram. The work thus indicated proceeds, with the changes in method already described, from the age of 5 to about 9. It is difficult to state a definite age by which certain stages will have been reached as so many factors contribute: class ability, the rate of progress of the individual within the class, richness of facilities, number of lessons per week, quality of teaching, etc. If the children experience a change of school at 7 (infant to junior) this is a useful opportunity for reassessing their ability and concentrating once more on their body management (control), especially in transferring (travelling) and receiving (landing and rolling) weight.

The children should be seen travelling freely and with confidence on both floor and apparatus. If this is so, progression can then take place as follows:

1 Apparatus

(a) The apparatus can be made more challenging for the children by greater use of sloping sufaces and by heightening and narrowing those which are horizontal.

(b) Work on the apparatus can be made more demanding if the

tasks aim at making the children more selective, for example, by suggesting that they find the most useful (best, appropriate) part (parts) of the body for travelling in a certain way – 'to grip while travelling from one end to the other', 'to slide down (up)', 'to swing along', 'to take you from side to side'.

(c) If possible the children should be given the opportunity to arrange, or rearrange, the apparatus allocated to their group and even sometimes to select their own apparatus to develop work they have been trying on the floor.

2 Further Development of Known Work

(a) *Flight* should be further developed from the initial experience of the *five basic jumps* (see Work for the Legs, Chapter 6). Combinations of these can form sequences of rhythmic jumps on the floor or with small apparatus such as hoops, canes, ropes, individual mats: e.g. 'Run and leap, repeat several times', 'Bounce in and out of your hoop and make a high spring over'. Hands too can help in flight, so jumps involving hands and feet, especially of the 'pouncing variety' (see Chapter 6, Stage II, Introductory Activity (vii)), can also be developed on the floor and with small apparatus. As with feet, either one or two hands should be involved in these practices, e.g. 'Move about the room taking your weight from your feet to your hands with a spring and rebound', 'Bounce as you jump on hands and feet from side to side of the cane', 'Travel about on one hand and two feet, twisting so that feet come down in a different place' (the other hand should take a turn).

In each of the above (i.e. feet only, or hands and feet) small apparatus can stress the difference between body impetus for height (over a cane) and length (along a mat). This experience of flight as flying upward or forward in space is very closely linked with body shape. Practice of varied and changing body shapes in jumps is of great interest at this stage and provides the children with effective experience of flight: e.g. 'Run and jump into a curled shape in the air', 'Run and jump into a stretched shape in the air', 'Run and jump into a shape with legs stretched in front of you', 'Run and jump with legs lifted backwards (sideways)', 'Run and jump with feet wide apart (near together)'. Equally interesting and enjoyable is the work on landings which can now be extended to experiment with rolling, sliding and diving. These activities have already been experienced as a means of travelling, but the children should now try them with a run to find the different body surfaces which are suitable for the purpose.

Work on flight can be further progressed on and off, over and along, forms and large mats and then on to stools, boxes and similar parts of the agility apparatus.

(b) *Bearing of weight* can be made more demanding at this age. Earlier, the child has discovered his ability to bear weight on the largish flat areas (patches) such as bottom, back, front, shoulders, shins, hands. Revision of these matching pairs of parts can lead to exploration of unmatched pairs, e.g. hand and foot, knee and elbow. This may result in the discovery that some of the parts are small (points) and thus develop interest in bearing weight on a single part such as hip, shoulder, knee. From this follows the idea of bearing weight on more than two parts, e.g. two hands and one foot, two knees and two elbows, head and two hands. The question of balance arises and the children should be helped to discover the relationship between balance, body shape and size of base, and to experiment along these lines.

With his greater knowledge and increased body awareness the child, at this stage, can appreciate that body shape in stillness is not inert and drooping but possesses a lively alertness. Such a position can be used to start an action so that the idea of alertness is stressed, e.g. a task can be given to 'Start balanced on a body part and find an action to take you on to your feet'. The children should be coached to find the most effective action to get from the starting place (recovery). The reverse process should also be explored, i.e. to find the most effective action to lead into the held position (preparation).

(c) *Symmetry and asymmetry* have a strong attraction for this age group. Work based on this contrast can develop naturally from the bearing of weight on one part only, as in (b) above, where the children experience one-sided body shapes. Body awareness is so far advanced that the children can consciously produce lop-sided, or uneven, shapes and movements in travelling and jumping, while at the same time appreciating the evenness of symmetrical actions. This can be linked with locomotion where the body twists and turns, this experience of off-balance giving further inspiration.

(d) *Movement sequences*. Work under the heading Flight, dealing with rhythmic jumps with feet or hands and feet, and that under Bearing of weight, finding actions leading into (preparation) or out of (recovery) a held position, have introduced the children to *continuity of movement*. This is important, and should be progressed deliberately. It can be further emphasized by stressing the pathway in tasks on one piece, or two linked pieces, of apparatus: e.g. 'Make a zigzag pattern with your feet along the rope', 'Find a way of going over and under the hoop' (supported horizontally), 'Cross and recross the mat', 'Move diagonally over the mat and come back straight across', 'Go along the form and over the mat', 'Travel along the form going from side to side, jump high off the end and across the mat near to it', etc. This idea can be further developed on more pieces of apparatus in a group situation.

The children now possess, to a certain degree, the essential ingredients of a movement sequence or 'phrase of movement': starting and finishing positions (parts that can bear weight), appropriate preparation and recovery actions, locomotion and continuity of movement. At first their efforts will lack their normal spontaneity of movement as they will tend to think before moving. With practice this will correct itself, but of course the extent of this fault will lie in their readiness (based on sufficient previous experience) to meet this new challenge of joining together, in an appropriate way, several simple movements or positions, e.g. 'Starting with weight on feet, body curled, roll with a change of direction and fly into a jump which lands you near the floor'.

The sequence should be explored, refined, and then repeated a number of times.

Another common fault with beginners is that the sequence does not *move* but is a mere changing from one position to the next. The children must be helped to travel, first by the wording of the task and then by the teacher's coaching. Clarity should also be worked for.

The value of working on movement sequences is that they train movement memory, make the children more selective, increase fluency of movement and give satisfaction through creativity.

3 Extending the Scope

(See Analysis of Movement, Fig. 1.)

(a) *Quality of Movement*

Having been up to now mainly concerned with action, the children become at this stage more aware of quality in movement. Therefore tasks on the floor and on apparatus should help them to develop this interest by dealing with *movement ideas* which bring out the content of the movement. These can be used in one or two parts of the lesson or taken right through a lesson, or series of lessons, in which case we say that the lesson or series is based on a *theme*.

Movement ideas such as these can be taken from the analysis:
    using different directions;
    changing directions;
    change of time;

accelerating and decelerating;
contrast in level (link with flight);
whole body – curling and stretching;
          twisting and turning;
          near and far;
          body shape;
awareness of different parts of the body;
parts of the body – symmetrical and asymmetrical,
          lifted high and lowered,
          together and apart,
          leading.

If the movement idea is developed from the floor training as a theme the tasks on the apparatus are *movement tasks*. In the action tasks used at an earlier stage the apparatus sets the problem ('Move *along* the plank') but, at this more advanced stage, what the children do on the apparatus depends upon the movement idea being explored: e.g. 'Move along showing a curl at some point and jump off with a stretch', 'Get on sideways and come off with a turn', 'Twist into the hoop and roll out', 'Roll along the apparatus'.

(b) *Partner Work*

Working in a group being now an established thing in the gymnastic lesson, the primary child can begin to work with a partner. Not only does he find this very interesting, but it fits with his psychological development. From his partner work his movement education gains impetus, for he learns new ideas from his partner, he learns to adapt his movement to his partner's movement and body, and he learns to observe carefully and then perform accurately. Lastly he gains social training in co-operating, leading and following. The stages in partner work suitable at this age are:

(i) *Matching* One partner copies the shape, pathway, movement of the other (a sequence of progression to be worked through in this order) whilst working one behind the other, side by side, facing, towards and away from each other (another progression to be worked through).

(ii) *Using a partner as an obstacle* One makes a supported shape (bridge or balance) and the other finds a way of getting over, under, around or through. There is challenge for the first in making his position original and more demanding, and for the mover in fulfilling the task *without contact* with his partner. At a further stage the obstacle may move too.

(iii) *Contrasting* Similar to matching, but with contrasting body shapes, pathway and actions. This can be related to (ii) above where the mover can be asked to produce a shape in contrast to that of the obstacle: e.g. obstacle in a stretched bridge shape and partner rolls through in a curl.

Progression in the three sections dealt with can take place concurrently and should provide enough material to complete the primary stage of education. At the end of this stage the children should not only 'be seen travelling freely and with confidence on both floor and apparatus' (see page 57), but they should be meeting the challenge of varying tasks and apparatus arrangements with versatility, initiative and thoughtfulness.

Chapter 9

The Primary Programme (continued) –
Play Interests at Different Ages – Play Theories –
Values of Play

PLAY INTERESTS AT DIFFERENT AGES

A number of theories have been put forward to explain why children play, but whichever theory is considered to be the clearest or fullest explanation, the play impulse is a factor in education which no teacher can ignore or neglect. The powerful impulse to play is innate in every normal, healthy child, and enables him to express himself. It drives him continually to experiment, to find out new ways, to try fresh things, because everything is a matter for curiosity and worth the expenditure of energy and interest.

PLAY INTERESTS AT DIFFERENT AGES

The play impulse shows itself in differing and developing activities as the child follows the regular process of growth, so that the play interests alter to keep pace with enlarging abilities and thus stimulate still further development.

For example, a child just at first may be satisfied with catching a bean bag, but soon prefers the greater challenge of a ball. He then finds harder and more varied ways of showing his mastery over the ball, throwing it up and jumping high to catch it, or juggling with more than one ball. As he develops strength, mobility and skill he enjoys competing with others in a group and still later in a team. (See 'Moving and Growing', Chapter 4.)

It is usual to classify play interests roughly in accordance with four periods of school life, but the line dividing any one period from the next above or below is in no way defined, although the difference between the play interest, for instance, of a child of 4 and one of 14 is clear cut.

Period I

Approximate age 1 to 7 covers the nursery school and infant school age. Play is individual, experimental, imaginative and imitative. The period is one of great emotional change.

The nursery child of 3 is completely interested in himself and what he can do, and he is not greatly interested in what other children can do. He is not interested in his own effort in any critical way. He does not specially want to improve, nor does he see any need for it. The fact that he manages, for example, to throw up a ball, though not to catch it, or to walk along a wide low form or wall, is enough.

By the time the child has reached 6 or 7 he is interested, though not in any detailed way, in what other members of the group can do. He can learn to take his turn in the group and to work with others.

Infants, in their play, need almost ceaseless activity of a massive undetailed type, such as running or jumping. They can be very vigorous for short periods of ten to twenty seconds on end. All-in races are therefore useful at this stage, probably incorporating an activity they have been practising, e.g. running, hopping or pat-bouncing a ball. Infants do not yet understand, or care for, games with detailed rules, nor can they wait very long for the climax of a game.

Infants enjoy repetition of activities already known to them. They enjoy feeling their power to use the body. This pleasure in repetition shows the more conservative side of their development and compensates them for the constant drive of their play interests.

Children of this age like to experiment on their own with apparatus, partly because they enjoy the handling of it, but also because they are hungry for skill. This is catered for, from the nursery school up, by frequent opportunities for playing freely with small apparatus such as bats, balls and hoops. The children still require the teacher to encourage and help individuals, first to develop their own ideas, and then to suggest limitations which will make the challenge and interest greater.

In infant activity there must be, then, little call on either sustained attention or physical endurance. At first, vigour and not skill is the keynote of the work, but there can be a steadily increasing opportunity for more finely controlled movement.

The play of Period I exemplifies the *surplus energy theory of play*. This theory looks upon play as the using up of 'the superfluity of energy over and above that required for the essential needs of life' (Colozza). According to this theory all the higher aesthetic feelings and artistic development arise as the result of the play impulse and this would seem to be important educationally.

Period II

Approximate age 7 to 9: Play is still largely individual and selfish, and self-assertion is strong.

Within certain limits the child should be provided with opportunities to give vent to the self-assertion which is the play characteristic of this stage of development.

The control of the muscles by the nervous system, that is neuro-muscular skill, increases so that big balls are handled and caught easily, and there is greater agility, both mental and physical, in dodging-type games. Systematic 'marking', however, such as comes in many team games like football and netball, is a much more difficult achievement and requires a more mature mental outlook.

Children of this age will try to play adult team games, such as cricket, because they like to feel grown-up, but there is little inclination to merge into and work for a group and not for self. Permanent dislike for games such as cricket or football may result if children are forced to play them this early.

Physical endurance and attention are greater than during Period I so that games can be longer. The climax, however, still cannot be long delayed, particularly as ideally each should have a turn as the chief performer in order to satisfy self-assertion.

Period III

Approximate age 9 to 11 +: The interests of this and of the preceding period merge largely into each other. There is a gradual change from individual self-assertive activity to that of group play under a leader. Play becomes realistic and competitive, evolving from individual to group competition. The relative abilities of others seem of more importance. There is interest in abstract records and a tendency to hero-worship, following the doings of popular footballers and cricketers not personally known to the worshipper.

At the beginning of this stage, a game involving the personal combative element, such as netball or football, easily makes players feel pugnacious. *Self-assertion* overcomes weak group feeling and play becomes angry and recriminative. The control of emotions that is involved in being able to play hard, be beaten and still really believe in the goodwill of opponents is a later development and one that does not grow of itself, but needs fostering.

Competitive work becomes of real interest and rivalry is strong. The competitive elements must, however, be simple and easily understood, and the result not too long delayed. Relay races, in which all competitors in turn perform the same activity, are characteristic of the spirit of competition in the *later stages* of this period, rather than team games such as football and netball, in which different players have dissimilar but complementary work to do for the team.

If relay races are used it is important that teams should be small, that there should be strict fairness in carrying out all competition, and that no result should be counted that is not fairly won. A frequent minor difficulty arises when a keen child edges over the starting line behind which he should stay until released by the previous runner. The teacher needs to point out briefly and good-humouredly that to do this lessens the distance the team has to run and so makes getting home first no gauge of success.

Play has become realistic, and imaginative activity makes no appeal. Children at this period need the quiet but firm guidance of an adult who will suggest activities and set a high standard of conduct and achievement. Skill and strength increase and a real, not imitative, interest in athletic competitions and sports appears.

Thus at this stage it is suitable to prepare children more specifically for the major games of Period IV by practising the basic skills in a game-like situation – e.g. dribbling, kicking, heading for football – and playing a miniature form of the game with small sides – say three against three, building up to bigger teams and learning the rules gradually.

During this period girls are physically more nearly matched in height and weight with boys than at any other time of their lives. Boys and girls should play together unselfconsciously, but the sophistication of town life makes for an undesirable division of the sexes for games at about nine years of age.

The *practice theory of play* is well illustrated by this period. The theory suggests that the origin of play is instinctive and that it has evolved as the way in which the young animal can test and practise its crude powers and learn in the safety of make-believe, where mistakes both of conduct and skill bring little penalty.

Period IV

Approximate age 11+ onwards: During this period growth quickens and emotions and interests of the sexes branch apart.

Girls mature earlier than boys and their attitude to play is the more sophisticated and detached. They will put up with poor, dull teaching more patiently than will boys, and the fact that they are more passive and have less kinetic energy available means that they are, perhaps, less easily enthusiastic about games. This does not mean that games, either for their physical, emotional or character-forming effects, should not be played, but the games chosen and the presentation should be specially suited for girls. Older girls of school age are often expected to help a great deal in the home, a call on energy that is much less for most boys. For both sexes there are, during this play period, greatly increased powers of endurance and control, but a more definite reason for activity is needed. Games that employ real skill and endurance, and in which the final result is delayed, for instance, for half an hour to an hour, are felt by the adolescent to be of interest and worth the output of energy.

Co-operative play involving team work under a leader is characteristic of the interest of the period. In hockey, for example, temperament and skill differentiate sharply between the players best suited to act as goalkeeper and centre forward, and to a lesser degree between those suited to play in the forward line as centre or wing.

The team still works together, but not all doing the same work, as in the earlier form of team competition. This involves the individual player in a recognition of other people's capacities and then a sacrifice of personal preference in favour of the best choice for the team's good.

Out of this co-operative play arises the subordination of self and of the earlier bias towards self-assertion in the interest of team play and loyalty to the chosen captain.

Ball games characteristic of this period involve the propelling of a ball either by kicking, throwing or striking with some form of bat or stick. All the major games – cricket, tennis, football, golf, hockey, handball, netball, rounders, stoolball – come into this class, together with numerous minor team game variations. Such games are characterized by fairly intricate rules which govern and standardize the play. These games exact from players a combination of physical vigour and alertness, quick co-ordination of hand and eye, stamina and resourcefulness. In addition, the players' critical ability and appreciation of skill become keener and thus personal achievement is stimulated.

Such team games give outlet for the primitive emotion of satisfaction in combat, in pitting strength against strength, speed against speed, skill against skill.

PLAY THEORIES

The *recreation and relaxation theories of play* accord better with the play of adolescents and adults than with that of younger children.

In the *recreation theory*, play is considered as a method of recuperation, as a way of drawing on fresh resources of energy after the mental and physical fatigue of work. The *relaxation theory* regards play as the temporary reversion to a simpler type of activity as a release from the strain of adult occupations.

The *recapitulation theory* of play supplies an explanation for the difference of play interests at different ages. The theory postulates that, in play, each young individual passes afresh through the ordered stages through which the race has developed – animal, savage, nomad and tribal for instance. The practice and recapitulation theories are not incompatible but complementary. They provide a biological explanation of play in contrast to the physiological explanations of the surplus energy, recreation and relaxation theories.

A third biological theory, which fills out still further our explanation of play, is the *cathartic theory*. It reminds us that play provides a wholesome outlet for excessive emotions. For example, we work off some of our love of power by developing mastery over a ball. We liberate our inborn aggressive tendencies by striving against our opponents in a game.

VALUES OF PLAY

Play has suffered in the past from being considered frivolous and trifling. While the mechanical and biological theories of play are all helpful to the teacher, probably the most valuable to him is the psychological theory. This asserts that play is joyous, spontaneous activity and it stresses the fact that it is an end in itself, whether reminiscent of the past or suggestive of the future, whether providing an outlet for surplus energy or for relaxation and recreation after the more strenuous efforts of everyday life.

Physically, play promotes growth and general nutrition by massive exercise which, as the child's powers develop, becomes more skilful. In play, the child puts forth his utmost strength and feels satisfaction in doing so, but he is protected in the early stages from becoming over-tired by a natural switching of attention and interest.

Educationally, play is the child's chief means of self-expression and it also helps his self-adjustment to the group. Through play, he should also gain increasingly in courage, grit, endurance and determination.

A quick reaction to external stimuli is of enormous importance throughout life. To dodge and to follow the dodger, to take in and act upon suggestions quickly, to realize that the ball is coming, decide how to catch it and direct the muscles to the final triumph of co-ordination in a successful catch are but a few examples of useful reactions experienced in play. The slow, clumsy child becomes more agile and expert in these directions, and thus more self-confident and willing to join in what he enjoys, thus increasing his opportunities to develop *neuro-muscular control* through play.

It has been said that one sign of neurotic personality is inability to accept the limitations of the material world, as for instance when rain comes and prevents a much-anticipated outing. Through play, the developing child meets and adjusts himself, with increasing philosophy, to this limitation of the material world. He learns to accept without fuss that it is not the bat that will not hit the ball, but the batsman who lacks the skill to do so. *The child learns to accept necessary frustration without wasting undue emotion on the matter.*

Socially, play helps to teach the child, while he is young enough to learn, what is his relative importance in relation to others, how to co-operate pleasantly, and the value of doing so in games.

To boast of success or to elaborate on the unfairness of non-success are equally unsocial. Although 'good manners' and 'good form' sound priggish when mentioned baldly, they depend on the ability of the well-controlled adult to inhibit his first feelings, to stifle a spontaneous tendency for disparaging laughter, the inclination to crude criticism, the commenting on personal peculiarity, the facile loss of temper. Play, and particularly the more skilled and organized team game, gives the child the chance to practise and appreciate such control, so that it is not just a pious theoretical aim, but a practice that operates even in the emotional excitement of a game.

Significance for Physical Education

If we have in mind the fulfilment of the child's potential in physical skill and movement, it is important that the selection of material in physical education should accord with his play interests at all stages. Only thus will we be assisting him to achieve his greatest possible skill and agility. Relationships and the ability to co-operate generally will benefit too from presentation and organization which recognizes the gradual change from the infant's self-interest to the adolescent's interest in the team.

Chapter 10

The Primary Programme (continued) –
Games in Primary Education (Stages I, II and III)

GAMES IN PRIMARY EDUCATION

Games spring from the same movement root as gymnastics, the functional and skilled action of the body in an objective situation. But whilst educational aims and values are frequently claimed on behalf of gymnastics there are fewer and fewer teachers ready to support the inclusion, in the programme, of games as a means of education. At the most, their merit is assessed in terms of 'an outlet', although reference to the previous chapter should make it quite evident that, to the child, play is not just an aimless release of surplus energy and high spirits. Play in fact 'never ceases to be a major business throughout childhood. Nature plants strong play propensities in every normal child to make sure that certain basic needs of development will be satisfied' (Gesell and Ilg), and high amongst these is the maturation of his natural skills.

If in the past children have not received valuable education through the games situation it is because the approach was wrong. Far too often the concern has been with teaching the games, rather than fulfilling the needs and interests of the children. The state schools, long ago, accepted a 'watered-down' version of the public-school system of games training and this permeated to the lower age groups. Any games training existing in infant and, especially, junior schools has been magnified to 'major' game proportions too early and too rapidly. Instead of starting where the child is, with a strong interest and desire to explore the excitement and unpredictability of a ball, teachers have organized large teams of primary children to ape adults in their attempts to play full-scale games of football, netball, rounders. This is surely indicative of the wrong approach mentioned earlier and it should be obvious that the time should be spent in activity based on the characteristics of children at the primary age and stage. Otherwise, we fail to make capital out of the child's instinctive and natural interest in what is later to become the focal point for him of all major games: the ball. This interest should be nurtured and coached into skill.

Meanwhile, the interest boys and girls have in the major games, at any rate before the age of 9, should be allowed to manifest itself in the children's versions of these games. The playing of these should take place outside the school timetable, spontaneously and quite free from adult organization and interference. Furthermore, the fact that a group of 8-year-old boys organize a game of football or cricket on the green in the evening should not be taken as proof that they are ready to play full-scale versions of these games as part of the school programme. The contribution the school can make to such natural interest and activity is in the proper provision for the development of the children's maturation skills and, at the proper time, coaching in suitable basic techniques.

The adult can see for the primary child the distant objective of a major game and may have in mind such ideals as character training, widening the scope of secondary school physical education, education for leisure, post-school recreation, but this is what it looks like from the top and it is therefore beyond the understanding of the child. His present needs should not be sacrificed to a future stage. Froebel says 'he is much injured and weakened by having placed before himself, at an early period, an extraneous aim for imitation and exertion, such as preparation for a certain calling or sphere of activity. The child, the boy, the man indeed, should know no other endeavour but to be at every stage of development wholly what his stage calls for.'

The present-day approach to games at the primary stage takes into account the importance of serving the children's present needs. What the primary school child needs, which the games situation can provide, is a wealth of experience with a wide range of small apparatus, especially balls of all sizes. With these he should be encouraged to practise and acquire the basic skills of all games, without undue emphasis on technique, which generally speaking should develop as an outcome of his play rather than precede it. This early training should be a period of fun, exploration and repetition fitted to his natural curiosity, his hunger for skill, his boundless energy and the fascination a ball holds for him. Bound up with this is the development of body control, so important in games, and basic also to his movement experience in gymnastics and dance.

Games Training

The word 'training' has become one to avoid, as it conjures up the idea of formality, maybe on account of its connection with the poorest type of physical training. In the present context, however, it is properly used to mean the logical development of the skill and stamina applicable to games, and not to indicate a formal approach.

The games training lesson should take place outside, on the playground or field, where the children have the advantages of freedom of space and fresh air and can acquire the healthy attitude of associating leisure with out of doors. To take such a lesson in the hall is frustrating to the children because of lack of space to try really hard, care lest lights are broken, losing of balls behind radiators or furniture, to say nothing of the distraction caused to other classes and teachers by necessary noise (e.g. repetitive ball-bouncing). Children should, however, learn to take care of equipment so, if the playground is wet, it is better to substitute an indoor gymnastics or dance lesson and take the first opportunity of putting in the missed games training on a day when small apparatus will not become wet and muddy from the playground surface. It should also be possible in the summer term to compensate the children for any great number of games lessons missed during the winter months because of consistently inclement weather, such is the importance of this opportunity for the primary child to develop his skills.

Apparatus

Enough apparatus should be available in boxes or baskets (see Chapter 6) for each child to have a hoop (suitable to his size), a skipping rope, a round-faced bat (small table-tennis type for the younger children, increasing to padder size and weight for the 7-year-old), a bean bag (for reception age), a small rubber ball for bouncing, a larger ball (not too heavy) to kick and head, and a perforated plastic ball to strike with the bat. In addition, for group use, there should be a number of large rubber balls (a dozen), a supply of skittles and canes, and some longer ropes for group skipping.

Seasonal Activity

Choice of activities should be appropriate to the season and weather. The handling of small balls is difficult for small, cold hands, so practice of skills of the rounders or tennis type would be inappropriate in winter time, whereas handling, kicking and aiming with larger balls would be suitably vigorous and warming.

Changing

Stripping should be as complete as for gymnastics, with the addition of a warm jersey if the day is cold, but fine and dry enough to play outside. The children will benefit from the more vigorous activity which results from taking off the bulky layers of clothing usually restricting their movement. Pliable, rubber-soled shoes are absolutely essential for safe play outside.

Preparation of the Playing Space

With the children's help, apparatus should be collected (in boxes or baskets), clearly sorted and arranged around the playing area so that each child can collect and return his apparatus without waste of time and risk of accident. If the playing space is too large the children may scatter too widely and thus be unable to hear the teacher's voice. This may be especially so on a windy day, though the teacher will have considered the extent of the wind in relation to the age and size of the children before taking them out, as skill and interest can suffer under such conditions. The teacher may, if absolutely necessary, use a whistle out of doors providing that he consistently uses it to mean stop, and does not *over-use* it. Otherwise, it is best to keep the class within sight and sound by restricting the playing area with a chalked line, a row of apparatus (e.g. hoops), or even for the teacher to place himself as a barrier between the children and the larger space. The latter is not an easy restriction to operate and it very much limits the teacher's contact with the boys and girls and his influence on their play. A blank wall of sufficient height, in conjunction with the playing space, is an asset and may be usefully marked with wickets, circles, etc. for aiming practices. Lines on the playground, especially down each side (a safe distance away) are also of value.

Application of the Movement Principles

The content of games training derives from:

1 The child's natural actions, his means of locomotion about the space using his feet. This use of feet is basic to the movement about a court or pitch in games. Versatility is developed by applying to his footwork the variations of time and space which he is meeting also in gymnastics and dance.

2 The child's growing awareness of his body and especially the actions of parts such as hands, feet and head. By applying to this his increasing understanding of the use of space, he easily adopts proper stance and the correct shape and size of a swinging action in propelling a ball or turning a rope.

3 The child's instinct to propel, and thus draw a reaction from, a ball. The matter of propelling involves the use of hands, feet, head and other body parts, and in then attempting to catch, or catch up with, the rolling or bouncing he has produced. He is helped in his control of the ball and his impact on it by increasing his manipulative (mainly gripping) skill through using other small apparatus.

In presenting the apparatus situations and suggestions to the children at this stage we accept that each child has his own natural ability and potential which we encourage and help him to develop. No standard is set, thus no child should suffer from lack of success and be dubbed 'a duffer at games'. This early success is important both to the child's present progress and his future attitude to games.

The phasing of games training follows the children's social and skill development as in gymnastics:

STAGE I: EXPLORATORY

This introduction to a games situation and the apparatus involved may roughly coincide with the reception period in the infant school. The lesson is appropriately simple:

1 Introductory Activity

As suggested for the gymnastics lesson, the children are introduced to the space through running. The experience is rather different because of the contrast in surface and the exhilaration of being out of doors.

The main aim of the activity is to encourage light footwork, response and good use of space, thus the same coaching points may be used as in gymnastics. Awareness of space can be further developed by running and stepping patterns, jumping for height and distance, galloping sideways and forwards.

2 Free Play with Apparatus

The children should be trained in the fetching, carrying and care of apparatus by simple rules:

(a) Always go to the nearest box;
(b) Carry apparatus carefully, especially when passing someone else;
(c) Find enough space to play in;
(d) Put apparatus down carefully and quietly;
(e) Return one piece of apparatus before taking another;
(f) Report any loss such as a ball over the wall.

Suggested Task: 'Get a piece of apparatus and play with it.'
Coaching: 'Keep moving.' 'Use all the space.' 'Be sure you have enough space to play in.' 'Can you find a different way to play with your apparatus?' 'Are your feet joining in the game by moving about your space?' 'Try the other hand.' 'Change to another kind of apparatus.'
Observation: The teacher, meanwhile, will be assessing the potential skill of individual children and encouraging effort and ideas.

3 Collecting Apparatus and Carrying it in to School

This should include checking to see that everything is in the boxes. Everybody should help to find stray pieces of apparatus, such as balls.

STAGE II: DEVELOPMENT OF SKILLS

AGE 5+ TO 7 YEARS – LESSON PLAN

1 Introductory Activity

This is the warming and limbering part of the lesson and, as in Stage I, it continues the early training in use of the space. Closely linked with this is the development of footwork and body control. The skill with apparatus later in the lesson will benefit if, in the introduction, the children can concentrate on feet, space and playing surface without the extra attention needed to grip a bat or rope or anticipate the reaction of a ball.

The ingredients of good footwork and body control are strong, agile feet and strong legs. These qualities will be acquired from such tasks as:

(i) Run quickly without touching anyone.

(ii) Run making patterns (shapes, figures, letters) with your feet.

(iii) Make a pattern on the ground, picking your feet high up.

(iv) Run and stop quite still (freeze) on the signal.

(v) Look for a space and run to it – *quickly*!

(vi) Run, changing direction on the signal.

(vii) Run and jump high in all the spaces.

(viii) Run and jump and land quite still (freeze) on the signal.

(ix) Run slowly and change to fast running.

(x) Run quickly and gradually change to running slowly.

(xi) Run, changing speeds.

(xii) Leap from foot to foot in all the spaces.

(xiii) Run and jump with a turn and land facing the opposite way.

(xiv) Run and jump with a turn and run in that direction – repeat.

(xv) Jump in all the spaces on two feet.

(xvi) How far can you go with one jump on two feet?

(xvii) Hop about the space on one foot, changing feet when one is tired.

(xviii) See how far you can hop on one foot before it gets tired.

(xix) How far can you go in one hop? Beat your own record. Try the other foot.

(xx) Travel about making a jumping pattern, sometimes using one foot and sometimes two.

(xxi) Skip about lightly making patterns.

(xxii) Skip as high as you can. Use your arms to lift you high off the ground.

(xxiii) Dodge into all the spaces from one foot to the other.

(xxiv) Run in a swerving pattern.

(xxv) Try jumping sideways on two feet – now the other side. How far can you jump sideways?

(xxvi) Move forward with a very long step. Try that in other directions. Now make a pattern stepping in all directions with long steps.

2 Skill Training

Although the children's play with the apparatus will still be exploratory and experimental, they can be helped to develop skills as these arise. The teacher can only fulfil this aim if he is aware of the natural development of the basic skills and can provide the sort of situations favourable to their progression. He will find it easier to promote the progression if each child is working with the same apparatus (as in a class activity – Chapter 6 on gymnastics) which can be changed once or twice in the time available to give variety. Progressions are listed for the various pieces of apparatus suggested earlier:

Bean bags

The duration of play with bean bags is short but they serve a useful purpose in developing some judgment in relation to catching, as they are more adaptable to the child's fingers, at first, than a mobile ball. This gives confidence for progressing to a ball.

(i) Free play with a bean bag.

(ii) Throw up and catch. Encourage and show, without actually teaching, the use of two hands to cup the bean bag.

(iii) Throw the bean bag away from you and chase it. Look for a space to throw into. Pick it up and repeat. Remind the children of spacing.

(iv) Walk, throwing the bean bag up and catching it. Develop running.

(v) Throw the bean bag over your head and turn round and catch it. Try doing that through your legs and turn round quickly to catch it.

(vi) Bean bag on one foot, hop about the space on the other foot. Change feet.

(vii) Develop any unusual idea seen in the children's free play.

Small balls with hands and bats

(i) Free play with a ball.

(ii) Roll the ball underarm and chase it.

(iii) Roll the ball underarm and beat it.

(iv) Roll the ball underarm and jump over it.

(v) Roll the ball underarm, jump over it, turn quickly and stop it with two hands.

(vi) Roll the ball against the wall and field it with two hands as it rebounds.

(vii) Throw the ball up and catch it (develop walking, then running).

(viii) Throw the ball up, let it bounce and catch it (develop walking, then running).

(ix) Bounce and catch the ball. Add low bounces, hard high bounces, walking and running.

(x) Pat bounce the ball continuously, low and high, in patterns around body, far forward, far out to the side. Pat bounce inside a hoop then moving round the hoop, changing direction. Change hands. Hoops away. Progress to walking and running about the space while pat bouncing.

(xi) Pat bouncing up into the air with either hand and do changes with pat bouncing down. Add bats and use plastic balls – the children enjoy the noise of the ball on bat and have their first real experience of 'striking'.

(xii) Throw the ball up against the wall and catch. This gives the basis of the underarm throw without teaching the stance or technique. Add spinning round before catching and how many claps before catching? Progress to letting the ball bounce before catching. Jump over it before catching from the bounce.

(xiii) Bounce the ball from the ground against the wall and catch it. Jump over it, turn round, clap hands before catching.

(xiv) Bat the ball away and chase it, stop it with foot, field it with hands, jump over it and turn round to field it, etc. Add bats and change to plastic balls.

(xv) Bat the ball continuously against the wall with hands then bat, develop by letting it bounce each time. Develop a 'rally'.

(xvi) Roll the ball at a skittle from about twelve feet. Field the rebounding ball.

(xvii) Aim overarm at the skittle – this will introduce the sideways stance and overarm action naturally.

(xviii) Throw the ball overarm into a space and chase and field it, etc.

(xix) Throw the ball underarm or overarm at the wall and catch or field.

(xx) Trick throws against the wall, round back, through legs, practice sequences (5 pats, 4 with a bounce, 3 through the legs, 2 round the back, 1 from ground to wall and clap before catching), etc.

(xxi) Juggling with more than one ball.

Larger balls with feet, head and other parts

(i) Dribble the ball walking, then running.

(ii) Dribble the ball in patterns, in and out of bean bags, hoops, etc.

(iii) Dribble the ball changing speed.

(iv) Dribble the ball changing direction.

(v) Kick the ball into a space and chase it.

(vi) Kick the ball against the wall and field it with two hands.

(vii) Kick the ball against the wall and trap it with one foot.

(viii) Kick the ball through a gap (bean bats, skittles) and trap it at the other side.

(ix) Dribble the ball and kick it through a gap, or at a target on the wall or a skittle, or into an inclined hoop.

(x) Head the ball and catch it. Find another part of the body which can strike the ball (knees, heels, elbows, shoulders, backs, etc.).

(xi) Keep the ball up with different body parts. Hands or fists may count.

Hoops

(i) Free play with a hoop.

(ii) Bowl the hoop and chase it. Turn to face it and catch it carefully. Jump over it (a small hoop) before turning to catch it.

(iii) Spin the hoop. Run round to see which stops first. Jump over it while it spins.

(iv) Bowl the hoop and dive through it as it turns. Develop by seeing how many times you can get through before it stops bowling.

(v) Jump over the hoop, in and out with two feet or one.

(vi) Jump backwards and forwards over a swinging hoop (held in two hands).

(vii) Skip in the hoop, turning backwards or forwards, with two feet together, one foot to the other, travelling about the space, etc.

Note: In all the ball, bat and hoop activities the children should be encouraged to try the practices with either hand.

Individual ropes

(i) Free play with a rope.

(ii) Jump over and along the rope laid on the ground.

(iii) Arrange the rope in a U shape and jump over, widening the gap.

(iv) Skip with the rope turning forward or backward, on the spot, feet together, one foot at a time, with a running skip moving about the space.

(v) Trick skipping, low down near the ground, pepper, double turn to each jump, cross the buckle, etc.

Canes and skittles

(i) Jump over the cane forward off one foot, two feet, with various body shapes, etc.

(ii) Jump over the cane with a turn.

(iii) Jump over the cane sideways using two feet, scissor kick, with a hop, with a hopping turn, etc.

Partners

When the children are skilled with the apparatus alone and ready to work with a partner, almost all the practices achieved alone can be further progressed with a partner. The teacher should be sure of this *readiness*, as the skill will suffer if the children resent having to share a piece of apparatus when they are still too concerned with their own practice to let a partner intrude. On the other hand, frustration arises if the practice remains too simple and needs the progression of a partner to revive interest. Examples showing partner progression:

Small balls (see page 77)

(ii), (iii), (vi) One rolls the ball and partner fields.

(ix) One bounces and partner catches, develop by running.

(x) In twos, keep the ball bouncing in a hoop, moving round the hoop changing directions.

(xiv) One bats the ball away and partner fields and runs in with the ball, or throws it in.

(xv) One bats the ball against the wall and partner takes the next strike and so on through a rally. When the ball is 'dead' partner starts with a 'serve'. Develop over a cane on skittles or a rope on small jumping stands.

(xvi) Two aiming at a skittle between them, fielding each other's shots. Progress aiming into a small hoop, then at a penny in the middle. Score.

(xix) One throws the ball under or overarm at the wall and partner must catch and then repeat. Score by losing 'lives'.

Larger balls (see page 78)

(i) One running and dribbling the ball and partner tries to take it and dribble away. Add dribble and kick the ball to partner.

(vii) One kicks the ball against the wall and partner must trap it.

(viii) One kicks ball through a gap to a partner who traps the ball and repeats.

(x) One heads the ball for partner to catch or trap or head back.

(xi) Keep the ball up in pairs using different body parts. Score.

Hoops (see page 78)

(ii) One bowls the hoop to the other who catches and returns.

(iv) One bowls the hoop and partner dives through.

(v) One holds the hoop horizontally or vertically and partner runs and jumps in or through.

Ropes (see page 79)

(iii) Beat partner's jump.

(iv) Two in a rope, facing or one behind the other, skip together.

Small Groups

Groups of 3 or 4 or 5 – several of the activities, especially with bats and balls or large balls, can be developed if the children are ready to co-operate. The group can also move on to longer ropes, two turning and one or two skipping in, running in to skip, skipping and running out, running through the turning rope.

3 Climax

The climax of the games training lesson can be:

1. *Top:* Travelling about the floor using hands and feet, *(bottom)* balancing on part of the body.

2. *Left:* Finding places on the apparatus where the body can   *(right)* the body can hang and curl too.

3. *Left:* Feet can help hands to hang, (*above*) other parts of the body can support the weight on apparatus.

4. *Right:* Large parts can bear the body weight, (*below*) small parts too.

(*right*) balance on or over the apparatus using other parts to help hands and feet.

5. *Left:* Travelling up and down the square ladder.

6. *Top:* 'Swimming' with a polystyrene float, (*bottom*) free play.

7. *Top:* Hands (*right*)-can
dance.

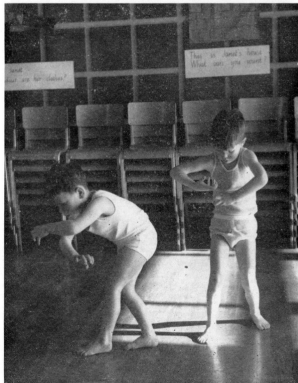

8. *Left:* A spiky dance, (*below*) dancing in a group with a percussion instrument.

9. *Left:* Contrasting shapes, *(right)* high and low.

10. *Left:* A small shape, *(right)* exploding!

. *Top left:* Hands and feet travelling along a form, (*top right*) bearing
partner's weight, (*bottom*) two make a gap the third travels through.

12. *Left:* travelling about the floor emphasizing feet high.

12. (*right and opposite page*) elevation and contrast in shape in jumping off a form.

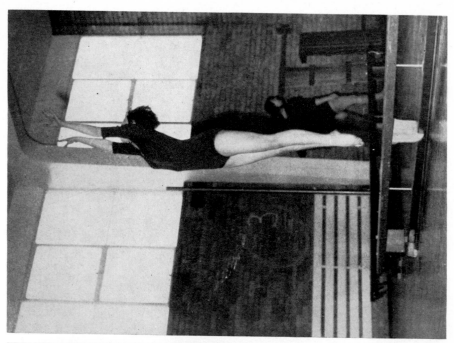

13.

14. Using parts of the body to balance and travel on form, beams and floor.

15. *Top:* Elbows move near to the body—(*bottom*) Work with a partner at a medium level.

16. *Top:* Using of hands at high level—(*bottom*) in preparation for a group dance.

Either (a) Free choice of apparatus so that some children may practise a favourite activity or continue with something they were enjoying or feeling successful at when the apparatus was changed.
Or (b) An all-in race using something already practised in this lesson or a previous one: e.g. running race, hopping race, hoop bowling race, pat bouncing race, two feet together jumping race, skipping race, etc.

Rules for Races

1 Run across the slope, if any, never down.
2 Have a starting line, though it is unwise to wait until *every* child is completely behind it before saying 'Go' as the children's enthusiasm makes them unable to wait so long.
3 Have a finishing line at least a yard from the wall at the other side so that the boys and girls have time to pull up.
4 Praise the general effort rather than picking out individual winners, (stand looking along the finishing line to see the finish) as the activity is more important to the children than the result, at this stage.

Or (c) Group work if this has been developing with various kinds of apparatus.

4 Conclusion

Collecting the apparatus, retrieving stray balls, etc., helping to carry everything into school.

STAGE III: LEARNING FUNDAMENTAL TECHNIQUES
AGE 7 TO 11 YEARS

If the children have a change of school at 7 (infant to junior) it is wise to spend a few weeks checking their ability by using some of the practices from Stage II.
Games training at this stage has to take into account three important aspects of the child's development:

1 A decided increase in motor skills and the gradual giving way of the maturation skills to the learning of fundamental techniques.
2 An increase in competitive spirit and the urge to compete.
3 An increase in strength, stamina and concentration.

Technique

By this time the maturation skills should have been helped to develop both by gymnastics and games training, and some promotion of certain of the acquired skills, such as throwing, catching, aiming and striking, should also have occurred. This now forms a sound basis for the more rapid development of fundamental techniques, e.g. stance, swing, grip, kicking with the instep instead of the toe, using a straight bat in cricket, etc.

Competition

The competitive urge is catered for by developing what was briefly indicated in partner work by the word 'scoring'. Throughout the practices suggested in Stage II, it was assumed that the teacher would encourage each child to beat his own record, see how many times he could skip (bounce, catch, etc.). With a partner the simplest form of competition was developed – *one against one*. Now at this stage the children can indulge their urge to compete and match their skill in more complicated situations. For example, skill in throwing and catching a large ball with a partner can be progressed to include a third child, who acts as defence, trying to intercept the ball (pig in the middle) and the organization is named *two versus one* (dribbling, kicking can be substituted for throwing). Further progression would produce a situation of *two versus two* (which would also apply to batting a ball and could bring in a net) and this could be progressed to *three versus three* when the children are ready for it. Competition can be catered for by some method of scoring, e.g. 5 consecutive passes without the ball being touched (or dropped) by the other side and you score a point, or a material means of scoring such as knocking down a skittle, bouncing the ball in a hoop, etc. The children can be helped to acquire a 'team spirit' by having coloured braids or bibs to wear.

Timetabling

As mentioned in connection with gymnastics, the children at this age can be so quick with their changing that it is possible to have the full timetabled time, which is usually 30 minutes, for the actual activity. In the first two years of this stage (7 to 9) 30 minutes' play is adequate, but from 9 years upwards the children can concentrate on their skill for longer and they also have the stamina to work wholeheartedly for 40 minutes. However, effort flags after this and there is no justification for timetabling juniors, of any age, for a 'double games period'. In fact, this is a denial of their right to a 'daily lesson' of physical education. Two single periods on two separate days give twice the enjoyment, practice and progress.

Timetabling problems are also created by separating the girls and boys for games at this stage in the primary school. This also is an unnecessary and uneducational arrangement since divergence of interest and ability is rarely marked at this stage. What is more, the games training programme makes it obvious that in this area of activity separation should not occur, for the children are being trained in the basic skills common to *all games*, not to be netballers or footballers. Any difference in interest can be catered for, in a mixed class, by different practices in group work and different group games developing from the basic practices. Many of the later problems in relationships could be avoided if we did not anticipate the segregation of the sexes in this artificial way in the primary school.

Apparatus

Additions to the apparatus are necessary: padder bats should be in full use now with the addition of padder tennis nets; also needed are small cricket bats or bat shapes; shinty sticks or, preferably, junior hockey sticks (Gray's of Essex now make these); small netball posts adjustable in height; portable wickets; sets of hurdles (make excellent goal posts for *three versus three* football or hockey); frido balls, or beach balls, for developing 'keeping the ball up'.

The plan is basically the same as in Stage II:

1 Introductory Activity

The work should be based on footwork such as running fast (for speed), running slowly (for endurance and stamina), running and jumping (to reach high balls), running and turning (to keep up with the game), running and swerving (for dodging), dodging over lines, in and out of hoops, etc. (for attack and defence), jumps of all kinds and skipping with ropes (for strong, agile feet and legs).

2 Skill Training

Individual, partner and small group (*two versus one, two versus two*) skill practices should be taken either consecutively as class activities or simultaneously as group activities.
Basic skills should be catered for:

(i) *Throwing and catching.* Various sizes of balls; various throws: underarm, overarm, bounce, over an increasing distance, stationary, on the move, with opposition; catching, basically with two hands, practice with one; fielding; juggling with more than one ball.

(ii) *Striking.* Padder bats, small cricket bats used both for cricket-like strokes and rounders-type swing, hockey sticks; in pairs, developing to threes with one bowling (develop from the underarm throw), one hitting and one fielding; padder tennis over a net; dribble and hit the ball to partner with a hockey stick; dribble and kick large ball to partner; defend wicket with a cricket bat while partner bowls; all progressed to working in fours.

(iii) *Aiming*. Aiming at various targets with various sized balls: rolling, overarm action, kicking, heading, shooting, bowling, hitting with a hockey stick; at targets on the wall, into hoops, at skittles, through netball rings (boys too for basketball).

3 Climax

This can be based on group work organization and should follow the theme of the skill training, in other words the children should be given an opportunity to apply the skill they have been practising in the lesson.

Either (a) Each group (four children is a suitable number) take the space and apparatus allocated, as for example:

(i) Cricket bat, ball and wicket, following skill training in striking a ball with a cricket bat, throwing the appropriate ball and catching and fielding.

Task: 'Make up a game in your group'.

The results may be games similar to 'Tip and run', 'French cricket', 'Hot Rice'.

(ii) One large ball and either a hurdle or a netball ring following training in throwing and catching, shooting at targets or through gaps and into hoops and rings.

Task: 'Make up a game in your group'.

The results may be *two versus two* 'football' or 'netball'.

When the children make up their own games they soon realize that rules are necessary if everybody is to have a share of the play and the apparatus. This is the moment for the teacher to begin giving basic rules, e.g. no rough play, a catch is out, etc.

Or (b) The teacher can present a game, based on the skill training, which each group can play *two versus two* or one player in and the other three fielding to get him out. Having explained the game and given *simple rules*, the teacher should put one child in charge in each group so that he himself can look at all the groups and give class coaching for common faults.

4 Conclusion

Collection of apparatus, retrieving stray balls, etc., helping to carry everything into school.

By the age of 10, skill should be high, technique with various balls and bats (sticks) well advanced, and the child should be socially developed and able to be part of a small team. Five-a-side games, based on the minor games (skittle ball, post ball, volley ball) and the major games (hockey, football, netball, rounders), and such games as badminton and deck tennis, will be possible. Games can be of longer duration for the children have more stamina by now which also means that pitches can be of a larger size (though not full size yet). A field is an advantage at this stage so that the 'games' can be well spread out and not interfere with one another. These group games, which involve simple organization (small teams and few markings) and few rules, ensure that all the children have equal access to the ball and share as much in the game as anyone else in the group.

At this stage the lesson plan may be adapted as the children are so keen to play the 'game'. This is catered for by starting with a game (in a class of 40 children four such games would be played), picking out those skills which need practice and explaining this to the children while promoting them as class activities or group work, then returning to the game for application of the practice achieved. Few children resent or deny the logic of this and are soon caught up in the idea of a better performance.

Competition may have developed to the point of inter-class games for the 10-year-olds but should not involve them in inter-school or league play because:

(a) There is a danger that the skill of the many is sacrificed to that of the 'team'.

(b) Those chosen to play are under too great pressure by having to win for the school, apart from the physical pressure of too large a pitch and too long a time to be fully exerted.

(c) Those chosen risk permanent damage to personality and nature by being pushed into an adult situation before they are ready for it.

(d) Those not chosen suffer degradation and a sense of failure which can have permanent results, if suffered at this particularly sensitive age, when personal skill and the regard of peers and teachers are so necessary to self-esteem.

Summary

When the child leaves the primary school the purposeful and enjoyable activity he has experienced in games training should result in his possessing the fundamental ability to play a number of group games successfully. These games have skills in common with the major games even though they have not demanded the high degree of co-operation needed in the full-scale versions of them.

Chapter 11

The Primary Programme (continued) – Swimming in Primary Education (Stages I and II)

In discussing games training it was suggested that it need not be justified in terms of the future. It is enough that we satisfy the present needs of the child. This can equally apply to the inclusion of swimming in the primary physical education programme. Although it is possible to discuss the values of swimming as an all-round physical exercise for adult leisure, as a family recreation, as a means of saving the life of a fellow human being, as a social grace especially for the adolescent, as a gateway to more sophisticated sports such as sailing and water polo, this is not the intention here. To be consistent in aiming to fulfil the child's present needs, all that requires to be said here is that swimming should be a necessary aspect of the young child's movement education because:

(i) It takes place in water, a medium in which he shows pleasurable interest from babyhood.

(ii) It is another form of functional activity satisfying his hunger for skill and enjoyment.

(iii) He can have fun swimming and if, at the same time, this makes him a more self-sufficient child, able to take care of himself in certain situations associated with water, this is also part of the primary school's general educational aim.

Swimming in education used to be fairly limited to the first-year children in secondary schools for several reasons:

1 It satisfied authority that at least an attempt had been made to ensure that children could look after themselves in water, which at this age increasingly comes within their experience.

2 Limited facilities (school baths, money for transport of children from schools to public baths, shortage of swimming teachers) made it impossible to provide swimming for all secondary children,

and if one age must be chosen this was as convenient as any, and more convenient than some, as it was already marked by transition.

3 Eleven was thought to be the best age to begin learning to swim, though 'readiness' was considered mainly in terms of buoyancy. This was rightly associated with the proportion in the body make-up of fat, which, having gradually decreased from walking age, increases just before the onset of adolescence. The latter commenced, on average, at about 11 years for girls and 13 for boys, and if the 'puppy fat' stage preceded it by a year, at respectively 10 and 12, an average of 11 years was deduced as the most buoyant age.

4 The time chosen interfered least with examinations, the girls and boys not being, as yet, vitally involved in 'O' level work.

The situation has changed for several reasons:

1 There has been an increase in the number of drowning accidents because of greater access by more of the public to water: sea, lake, river, pond; through easier travel: by train, bus, cycle, family car; and the greater incidence of family holidays.

2 The increased popularity of water sports resulting from access to water and interest created by television and newspaper coverage of world events.

3 Research in child development, and especially into 'readiness' and the learning of skills, has brought other factors into the consideration of what should be the best time to begin learning to swim. Eleven is now felt to be much too late, especially as the secular trend towards earlier adolescence has pushed the 'puppy fat' stage down into the primary school. Many experts in the educational field now choose 7 as the time when the child is 'ripe for learning', especially skills; and as skill in swimming can only be developed after confidence, it may never be too early to begin learning; as evidence there is Virginia Newman's startling success with teaching babies, aged 8 months and up, to swim.

4 The development of Purley pools and other learner pools. This cheaper and less extensive facility has greatly increased the provision of swimming teaching, especially in primary schools. Pools now exist on primary school premises: sited in a spare classroom, on a playground with windbreak protection, in a purpose-built hut or pavilion; or in a village hall; or in a central place shared by a group of schools. Thus, provision is made for children from the age of 5 years.

Advantages of Teaching Swimming in a Learner Pool

(a) Depth of water – the water is shallow and can be adjusted and made shallower according to the learners' ages and progress.

Recommended depths are:

5 to 7 years	1 foot 6 inches to 2 feet 3 inches
7 to 11 years	2 feet to 3 feet
11 + years	3 feet to 5 feet

The shallowness of the water removes fear and makes learning easier, for even the smallest children are not out of their depth and have no problem in regaining a standing position. The even depth of water is important too, for there is no shelving towards a deep end as in a public bath, though graded steps for entry are available and can prove very useful.

(b) The smaller expanse of water greatly reduces fear, and the size of the pool being installed can be related to the age of the children who will use it.

(c) The quiet atmosphere is in contrast to the resounding noise in the public baths. Noise can be frightening to younger children and disturbs the concentration of even the older groups.

(d) Siting of the pool on the school premises not only makes it familiar but has an added advantage in that the children can visit it and see others enjoying a lesson before starting to learn themselves.

(e) The numbers swimming at one time are limited by the size of the pool to a homogeneous group. This makes it easier for the teacher to teach and to supervise the safety of the children, whereas one of a group being taught in a public bath can easily be 'lost' in the crowd, with a possibly disastrous result.

(f) The temperature can be adjusted for each class, according to age if necessary, whereas it is kept at a point more suited to actual swimmers at the public baths. Also, the smaller area of water can be more economically heated to the higher temperature suitable for younger children.

(g) By having a pool on, or near to, school premises, time is not wasted in travelling and this also lessens the risk of chill after the swimming session.

Advantages of Teaching the Younger Children to Swim

(a) They have an intense curiosity for the pool as they associate it with the big bath at home, especially if, at first, the temperature of the water is similar. The children are therefore prepared to enjoy the experience and, because of the pleasurable sensation of being in water, to learn.

(b) Young children have no fear; this comes later as they learn a proper appreciation of the dangers of being immersed in a comparatively large bulk of water. They can be prepared for this time by being taught to swim before fear can develop.

(c) Their natural suppleness makes learning to move the limbs in water much easier than it becomes later in life when suppleness diminishes for various reasons.

(d) Fat is important for buoyancy and the proportion of fat to body bulk lessens from the age of commencing to walk until just before the onset of adolescence, when once again the body fills out and becomes plump. It would seem wise to take advantage of the buoyancy factor the first time round and introduce children as young as possible to the swimming situation so that they may develop ability (to float) which they will keep. Of course, strength in combination with buoyancy is important, but here again the child from the age of 5 years, with his sturdy body and increasing muscle power, is at an advantage.

Who Should Teach?

The class teacher is the most appropriate person, next to the parent, to teach a child to swim, for the close relationship inspires the confidence which is basic to this area of learning.

The teacher should, if possible, be able to swim himself so as to:

(a) Appreciate the sensations the child will have of the coldness of the water; its upthrust; the way in which it impedes progress by resistance; and the blurring effect it has on vision when the face is immersed; and

(b) Life save, if necessary, though in a learner pool this should only involve wading in; and be able to apply artificial respiration.

Teaching should take place from the bath side, except for the first lesson or two with the 5+ age group, so that the teacher can see every child; but he should be dressed ready to go into the water, if need be. It is useful to have a pole to give support to any child needing to be helped to the side of the pool. The teacher's voice should be quite adequate in the quietness of the learner pool and creates a better atmosphere than a whistle, the shrill tone of the latter shattering concentration by startling some of the children.

Length of Lesson

The lesson should not be too long, especially at first, as:

(a) It is difficult to concentrate for too long in the strange situation.

(b) The child quickly becomes cold as the body attempts to adjust to a medium which conducts heat more rapidly than air, though it is itself warmer than the air temperature.

(c) The activity is physically fatiguing as energy is being used, not only in the form of heat given off to the water, but also in the greater muscle power needed to move against the resistance of the water.

Therefore, to begin with, about ten minutes should be spent in the water, increasing to thirty minutes, as a maximum, at the top of the primary school.

Frequency of Lesson

Learning takes place more rapidly when practice is concentrated. Experiments with weekly versus daily lessons, at Ilford, Carlisle and Kilmarnock, have made this very clear with regard to swimming. Children make more progress if they have swimming every day for a fortnight rather than once a week for a whole term. If a daily lesson is not possible, then an attempt should be made, when teaching of strokes commences, to organize two or three lessons a week until the children can swim a length. This lifts them more quickly on to a 'plateau of learning' from which further progress can be rapid.

The Approach

It is best to delay the start of swimming lessons until the children know the teacher. Their confidence in the relationship transfers to the strange situation. For the sake of safety the teacher should have established control in the classroom and especially in other aspects of physical education which take place in the hall or playground. This ensures that the children will respond to his word or signal and listen to instructions. The children can be prepared for the commencement of their swimming sessions by looking at pictures, films, and slides and by watching and discussing the movements of the fish in the school aquarium. They should also visit the pool, at least once, to look around and see other children swimming and, if they are not to be taught by the class teacher, have the instructor introduced to them.

The teacher's attitude and manner are important to confidence; he himself should be confident and cheerful, and careful not to show any feeling of discouragement or apprehension. Praise is an important aid to progress in swimming, whereas to show disappointment when a child fails to succeed stunts the urge even to try again. A smile and a comment praising the effort can be most effective: 'Well tried! You'll manage that next time.'

A Code of Conduct

This must be established from the very first session at the pool:

(i) Good habits of hygiene, including toilet, shower and footbath routine. It is clean and safe for both girls and boys to wear caps unless the hair is cut short.

(ii) The teacher should be ready first so that there is no danger of a child entering the water alone.

(iii) No one swims who has an infectious disease, a sore spot, verruca, or athlete's foot.

(iv) No running on the bath side.

(v) No one enters the water before the teacher's signal.

(vi) No one enters the water with anything in his mouth: sweets, chewing gum, etc., can be washed into the gullet by an accidental mouthful of water and cause choking.

(vii) No horseplay or faking of accidents.

(viii) Dry quickly and thoroughly, especially hair and feet.

Organization and Progression

Assuming that swimming will be included in the physical education programme from the beginning of the primary school, the phasing follows the same pattern as for gymnastics and games, though it may be advisable to omit the reception stage because of the importance of children and teacher knowing and having confidence in each other.

STAGE I: EXPLORATORY
AGE 5+ TO 7 YEARS

This stage is based on exploration, enjoyment and fun. Each individual child, as in gymnastics and games, has his own aptitude and ability, therefore learning depends upon individual attention.

Water temperature should commence at 90°F. for the first few lessons, being gradually decreased, but should rarely fall below 80°F. during this stage.

The work suggested follows the *shallow water method* based on a learner pool. It is assumed that, if the children are taken to a traditional bath, the swimming instructor will be in charge of the teaching and the class teacher will only be required to supervise their changing and behaviour.

Depth of water should commence at 18 inches, though if the children are not soon 'waterborne' in this depth, it can be lowered to as little as 12 inches and, with progress, increased to 2 feet or 2 feet 3 inches. The number in the class should be no more than 20, so some organization may be needed to halve the normal class and leave one group in the classroom with the head teacher or an auxiliary, repeating the swimming lesson for this group at another time. The teacher will also need help at the pool while introducing the children to the (un)dressing and hygiene routines. If it is possible, each child should be equipped with a rubber ring, fitting well under the arms so that he cannot slip out of it. These are difficult to put on ready blown up, so it may take a little time to inflate 20 of them on the children, without help. The children become quite expert at self-inflating them as time goes by.

1 Entry

Just as the undressing, folding of clothes and hygiene routine have been taken in a calm and leisurely manner, so too should the entry to the pool be introduced. The children should not be rushed into the water, least of all on the first few occasions.

Suggested Introduction. All sit on the edge and dangle, then splash, feet; or on the top step of a stepped approach which gives the opportunity to move down a step and repeat the splashing until they are sitting in the water. If there are no steps of this type, form a crocodile, holding hands, with the teacher at the front, and he can lead the line down the ladder and into the water. Continue in the line walking about the space in the water – 'Follow the leader' – teacher leads the children in patterns. Make certain children into leaders and let them lead small lines – Coach 'Try not to bump anyone' (as in gymnastics and games) and 'Don't break another line'. Develop this activity to moving about the space alone and the children, meanwhile, will become used to the water resistance on feet and ankles, as well as beginning to feel 'at home' in a new kind of space.

2 Training

(i) Sit down in a space – check spaces, as room to swim will always be important, so this is a good habit to develop.

(ii) Splash feet – recheck spacing.

(iii) Splash hands.

(iv) Splash hands and feet. Some children will, probably as early as this, get a feeling of upthrust from the water and achieve their first experience of buoyancy.

(v) Lean back with weight on hands (a favourite position during story time in the classroom). Splash feet again – bottoms may lift off the floor of the pool, rings will support and some children will be buoyant – tell them 'You are swimming'. That is what they came to do and immediate success will breed further achievement. Encourage those individuals ready for it to put heads further back until ears are in the water and go on splashing feet and legs upwards and downwards. By adding splashing of hands, some children may propel themselves backwards (remind them of spacing). There is no problem about getting up from this supine position as the water is so shallow.

(vi) In spaces again, kneeling down facing the water and with hands flat on the floor of the pool. Push feet back so that legs are lifted and the whole body is on the water surface. 'Walk' on hands about the space. Push up on to finger tips. Some of the children will take finger tips off and find themselves floating. Allow time to experiment.

(vii) The teacher can prepare the children for the next stage by asking in the classroom if they know how a dog swims. Discussion, and the demonstrations forthcoming, will give each child at least a mental picture of 'dog paddling'. Following on the walking on fingertips in (vi), the suggestion to 'dog paddle', for which they have a natural ability, will successfully propel some of the children through the water. The mental practice resulting from being told to 'pull' through the water in front of them will reinforce their practice. A few children may instinctively splash their feet behind them and be actually 'swimming'.

(viii) Without it being stressed, some children will have accidentally put their faces into the water during the previous practice. This can now be promoted by kneeling in the water and splashing it up on to the face with two hands. Encourage them to bend nearer the water so that 'washing' is easier and, from this angle, most children will immerse the whole face in their enthusiasm. This is a much pleasanter experience than going under with chin, then mouth, then nose, then eyes, then top of head; because at the point where the nose is still free the child can still breathe in and risks taking splashed up water too, which is rather painful. With *both* nose and mouth in the water it is impossible to breathe in (a reflex beyond our control) so the method of immersing the whole face is safer and pleasanter.

(ix) Have some objects to drop into the water, one for each child, spaced out like the children. 'Can you see it in the water?' 'Tell me what colour it is.' Without thinking, most children will immerse their faces and open their eyes in the water to see the colour. This is very important, as it accustoms them to adjusting to the blurring of vision and to swimming with eyes open, which they will need to do in a public pool. Also they should get used to immersing the face for complete buoyancy and in order to save energy later on in breast stroke and front crawl. Encourage practice of immersing the whole face at home, in the bath or in a bowl of warm water.

(x) Practise picking up the objects with alternate hands.

3 Free play

For the last 2 or 3 minutes the children should play, freely, games suggested by the teacher, such as ring o' roses, submarines, mushrooms, star fish, crocodile walk, or games they invent themselves. For instance, if they have been rolling softly on the floor in gymnastics, it is probable that they may try this forwards or sideways in the pool. The teacher can help them to find names for their tricks, such as porpoise (forward) and turtle (sideways). Through their play, many of the children will find their own ways of propelling themselves through the water and this should be praised and encouraged.

Notes

(a) Objects referred to in (ix) should not be too small, rather have them too big, like quoits. Bone baby rings and coloured discs about 2 inches across have been used successfully. Marbles are not suitable as the children can slip on them and also want to put them into their mouths (see Code of Conduct).

(b) Inflatable arm bands may be used instead of rubber rings but they have disadvantages: there are two to inflate instead of one for each child, some children find them more uncomfortable and restricting on the arms than the ring is on the chest; if the arms are raised out of the water their effect is lost.

(c) The air in the ring should be decreased as the child shows progress, until at the right moment the ring can be taken off altogether. The right moment is in the middle of a lesson when he has propelled himself successfully through the water wearing a ring with little or no air in it. At this point he will remove it and repeat his achievement unaided.

Partners

When the children are at the stage of working in pairs, especially in gymnastics and games training, this can be introduced in the pool. It will probably coincide with an increase in the water level. One child holds his partner's hands and gently pulls him along in a prone floating position while his legs kick behind him making the water 'boil'. The experience of making progress throurh the water is important and should give the child an extra incentive to 'dog paddle', if he has not previously managed to do so.

Meanwhile, as already indicated, the depth of water should be increased in accordance with the progress of the class, and the temperature dropped as the children become more vigorous in their activity and therefore able to keep themselves warm.

STAGE II: AGE 7 TO 11 YEARS

Water depth may commence at 2 feet, as the children are now quite tall, but this is not the deciding factor because the 7-year-old may be more fearful of the water than he would have been at 5 years. Artificial aids should be used, starting with each child with a ring.

Aims of teaching at this stage are:

(a) To reinforce (further to the experience of Stage I) or establish (if the children have missed Stage I) *Confidence*, then

(b) to promote *Technique* (as in games training).

(a) *Confidence work may include:*

(i) Any of the suggestions from Stage I suitably adapted to the age and increased skill.

(ii) Holding hands in pairs, taking turns at 'ducking under'.

(iii) Holding the rail lying forward with face immersed, splashing legs. Repeat on the back.

(iv) Hands joined in circles of eight, numbered in twos. Ones and twos lie back on the water alternately. More support is given if those standing have feet firmly astride. Show and coach how to regain a standing position from back float: sweep the arms firmly down towards the feet, bending the hips back and pushing the head as far forward as possible. This is much easier to practise with the circle support.

(v) Repeat the above practice with ones and twos alternately lying forward on the water. Show and coach recovery to standing by sweeping the arms back and drawing the knees up.

(vi) Practice of back and front float recovering to standing as in (iv) and (v). This could be a partner practice, the partner being particularly useful in recovering from back float by helping to lift the head.

(vii) Push and glide on the front to a partner: kneel with back towards the side of the pool and toes in contact, stretch the arms forward in the water, breathe in, immerse the face and lie forward, gently pushing off from the side with toes. This should be a very effortless action and should carry the performer over increasing distances to his partner who can move gradually further away. Follow with recovery to standing.

(viii) Push and glide on the back to a partner: face the side with knees bent so that shoulders are submerged and hands at sides; lie back pushing off gently with toes. As the head goes back and ears submerge, the tummy should lift and the performer moves backwards over the water without effort to his partner. Follow with recovery to standing, partner assisting if necessary.

(ix) Mushroom float. Bend forward immersing the head, clasp both hands round the shins and bring knees up to chin. The body will float. Recover to standing.

(b) *Technique*

The next thing to develop is technique as the children at this age are 'ripe for learning'. This is probably the best time to begin to learn actually to *swim* as the child is relatively strong; has developed sufficient co-ordination; is still reasonably supple; and he has learned discipline and understands, and will listen quietly to, explanations.

Technique means *strokes* and the question is which stroke to start with. The answer is: let the child choose, thereby acknowledging the fact of individual differences of size, strength, suppleness, comfort (some children dislike at first having their face in the water, whereas others are loath to trust themselves back on to the water). This choice involves the teacher in the use of the *multi-stroke method* in which the children are shown the quick simple beginnings of the breast stroke and front and back crawls, which they try and from which each child makes his own selection. The children, now in three groups, copy the 'whole' stroke, then do practices of parts as suggested by the teacher, e.g. breaststroke leg kick with partner support or artificial aid (polystyrene float). After practice of parts, the whole stroke can be tried again. It is important to let the children try the whole stroke first as the parts are not meaningful on their own.

Detailed technique is not important at this point. What is important is that the child should feel the success of moving through the water, for he came to the pool to swim! The earlier in the period, 7 to 11 years, he acquires this skill the better the ultimate results will be.

The teacher is here involved in group work, three groups each doing a different stroke. Artificial aids are most important and useful.

(i) Polystyrene floats (balsa wood or cork are also available but are not so good). It is important with floats to coach 'Push away from you', because if the child pushes down into the water he will lose balance and go under.

(ii) Rubber rings, armbands, flippers, the latter being quite safe for this age group in the learner pool.

If preferred the teacher may adopt the *single stroke method*, the choice of stroke being either the teacher's preference or the result of considering the children's aptitude for front or back float. Traditionally, the stroke most often chosen was breast stroke, though this is not so usual nowadays when several arguments are raised against it:

(i) It involves the beginner in putting his face in the water, a sensation which he may still dislike.

(ii) The track of the stroke, leg and arm actions, is difficult to visualize because it is unnatural and not within the child's experience.

(iii) Timing and co-ordination are difficult.

(iv) Some children naturally lack the necessary suppleness of hip joints, for turning out, and ankles, for extending the feet.

Whatever the method chosen, the teacher is now involved in some simple stroke analysis so as to devise practices and help with arm and leg actions and timing. It is not intended to go into this in detail, as many simple and excellent books are available which will supply the necessary analysis. Also, it is assumed that the teacher can swim and therefore knows the structure and timing of the strokes.

Full use should be made of the rail for supporting feet or hands to practise parts of a stroke, and of the artificial aids, especially polystyrene floats for practice of leg actions and flippers to promote propulsion.

Breathing

This has not been dealt with as such, the theory being that if the child acquires the ability to submerge his whole face he will naturally hold his breath and then breathe when he lifts his head as part of the stroke, e.g. when the arm action raises the upper part of the body clear of the water in breast stroke. On his back, feeling completely confident and relaxed in the shallow water, he should breathe quite normally.

In learning strokes the child is helped by:

(i) Mental practice such as thinking of taking hold of the water or pulling on the water.

(ii) Some means of measuring progress which, having regard for individual differences, matches him against his own previous achievement rather than that of his stronger and taller peers. Thus, he can beat four widths of front crawl with five, etc., then go on to lengths; in this way building up stamina before he goes to a public bath and there reverts, temporarily, to widths at the shallow end. A.S.A. Survival Awards also come within the scope of the top end of the age range, by which time the depth of water will most probably be three feet. Also possible in shallow pools are the tests for the National Certificates (five Awards), inaugurated in 1967 by the A.S.A. and English Schools Swimming Association.

Entry

It is not necessary before this time to consider entry; the pool has

G

steps and the children have used them. The first priorities have been to get them 'waterborne' and swimming. However, on considering survival tests, entry to the water becomes important. With the greater depth (3 feet) of water now in use, practices in the learner pool can progress:

(i) Begin by sitting on the side and, putting both hands to one side, twist sideways and slide into the water. Repeat to alternate sides.

(ii) Begin standing on the side, step forward with one foot leading, body completely vertical, and raise arms sideways as you enter the water. The parted legs and raised arms prevent the body going too deep in the shallow water and thus eliminate jarring of the feet on the floor of the pool. It is absolutely necessary that the body be vertical on entry otherwise some body surface may painfully slap the water. Repeat the practice using alternate feet.

(iii) Begin standing on the side and step off, but tuck up with arms holding knees to chest for entry to water. This, also, prevents too deep an entry.

The Lesson plan for Stage II is basically the same as for Stage I.

1 Introductory Activity

Moving about the space in crocodiles, follow my leader, circle float, etc.

2 Technique Practice

Individual, partner or group practice of push and glide, recovery, mushroom float, strokes.

3 Free Play

The child can go on practising something he enjoys or is making progress with, work on stunts such as somersaults, handstands, underwater swimming, picking up objects, jumping in, treading water.

It is in this part of the lesson that the teacher may develop the basic ability to *dive* with *some* children. All have had the fundamental practices, immersing face, ducking, push and glide. Now those who can develop, through free play, a somersault in the water, can then try a handstand. A further practice combining push and glide and handstand can be made more meaningful if done in pairs, the performer aiming to go through the parted legs of his partner. This version of surface diving can be further developed in deeper water when the children are promoted to the public bath.

Land Drill

All mention of land drill has been deliberately omitted as it is felt that the carry-over from practice on land to performance in the water is negligible, because of the different medium. The same applies to demonstrations which should, if possible, be given in the water.

Further educational values of swimming:

Swimming is the complete exercise, involving every muscle in the body if the whole range of swimming is explored. It offers an opportunity for vigorous activity and yet, on the other hand, can be completely relaxing if the swimmer prefers to make the gentlest of efforts.

At the primary stage, swimming makes a special contribution to the weak and underdeveloped child who, at first ineffective, gains some strength from his puny efforts which, making him a stronger swimmer, gives him the ability to gain greater strength and stamina.

For the fat child too, swimming has a special contribution in that, being more buoyant than his fellows, this may be the one physical activity at which he can shine. The teacher's praise raises his prestige, an unusual occurrence for many a fat child, and he is spurred to greater efforts, thus giving his body the exercise it so much needs. It may not be possible to reduce his weight through swimming, but at least his muscles respond to the strenuous activity and he gains shape and poise.

Chapter 12

The Primary Programme (continued) –
Dance in Primary Education – Body Awareness –
Spatial Awareness – Dynamic Awareness – The
Sixteen Basic Movement Themes – Stimuli in Dance

DANCE IN PRIMARY EDUCATION

Dance is the aspect of movement education most often neglected in primary schools, in spite of being the oldest and most natural human activity. The child is born with the instinct to dance, thus its inclusion in the physical education programme should present no problem of appeal or interest, least of all at the primary stage.

Dance is the aesthetic form of excess motor energy; an art form antedating all other art forms; 'the mother of the arts' (Curt Sachs). Man experienced his original perceptions in this, the only activity calling upon the whole individual to use physical, emotional and intellectual powers equally and in unison. From this experience of the whole, man learnt to direct his creative urge into other expressive channels. It seems likely that the physical power of expression through movement gave origin to the graphic arts of writing, painting, drawing and engraving; the emotional expression through sound became tone and eventually music; while the intellectual expression developed through the medium of speech into prose and poetry.

In dance the intangible mood, idea or emotion can be expressed through the tangible, that is the body. Primitive man had an appropriate dance for every important happening in life. He danced to welcome Spring; to ward off evil spirits and to encourage success; to celebrate the festive occasions of marriage, birth and death; to reinforce the culture of the society. But through the centuries dance suffered manipulation, modification, suppression, sophistication, being ultimately confined to specialized moulds so that it became watered-down historical fact, a form of entertainment or a superficial social accomplishment.

In the early 1900s an era of revolution began: a rebellion on opposite sides of the world against the rigid forms of dance with highly specialized technique. Such personalities as Isadora Duncan and Rudolf Laban led the way to the freedom of dance. Laban, through his research into, and analysis of, human movement, evolved a philosophy built upon unassailable principles and, as a result, dance has been rediscovered and displayed in its original uncluttered form. Now too we have the advantage of an organized system of notation and the necessary jargon to record the artistic language of dance, to experience, to speak, and to write and understand the full range of movement in all its variety and richness.

The range of movement possibilities in dance is governed only by the structure of the instrument – the body – and the natural laws governing movement. These mechanical laws of motion, gravity, balance, force and leverage are common to all efficient movement. In dance, movement is used in all its possibilities and varieties, from the simplest forms to the most extravagant complexities, from natural everyday actions through symbolic patterns to abstractions, from spontaneous reactions to the sternest discipline.

The Basic Language – the Action – of Dance

To be able to communicate in movement it is necessary to experience and understand the language. This language falls into *three* groups.

1 BODY AWARENESS

The *first* group is concerned with body awareness, knowing '*what*' the body can do, being aware of its powers and limitations in the physicality of movement. Because of its skeletal and muscular anatomy the body can perform:

(i) three mechanical *actions*:

  (a) bend,
  (b) stretch,
  (c) twist;

and (ii) five basic *actions*:

  (a) gesture, i.e. a movement which does not involve a transference of weight,
  (b) locomotion or stepping, i.e. transferring of weight using the general space,
  (c) stillness, i.e. the use of muscular energy required to 'hold' a position,
  (d) elevation, including the five basic jumps,
  (e) turning.

From these actions certain basic body activities can be developed:

(a) opening and closing,
(b) advancing and retreating,
(c) rising and falling.

he structure of the instrument further affects movement in that can:

(a) be symmetrical (two-sided) or asymmetrical (one-sided), and
(b) occur in a simultaneous or successive fashion.

Body shape

The body can assume many different shapes classifiable into four basic groups:

(i)   One-dimensional, linear or arrow shape.

(ii)   Two-dimensional, spread flat or wall shape.

(iii) Three-dimensional, round or ball shape.

(iv)   Three-dimensional, twisted or screw shape.

The actions and shapes referred to can be applied to the body as a whole and to the various parts of the body.

2 SPATIAL AWARENESS

The *second* group is concerned with the pattern and shape of the dance, with knowing '*where*' the body can do '*what*', being aware of personal space and general space in an intellectual way.

Personal space is all that space within arm's reach at all levels and in all directions. There are three levels: high, medium and low; six basic directions: up and down, forward and backward, from side to side (Figure 6). The directions can be related to the three axes of movement as stated in mechanics; these intersect at the centre of gravity and, in dance, extended they form the dimensional cross.

Any two of the three dimensions put together form a plane or 'corridor' of space for movement: so the 1st and 2nd dimensions give the frontal or *door* plane, the 2nd and 3rd dimensions form the horizontal or *table* plane, and the 1st and 3rd give the sagittal or *wheel* plane. When all three dimensions are combined, diagonal pathways in space are produced.

The rhythmic pattern of dance in space can be disciplined into well-ordered crystalline shapes. Thus, arising from these diagonals, dimensions and planes we get a cube, an octahedron, an icosahedron. These points in space allow the body to experience full flexibility as it practises the scales of movement, the various rings and equators, moving peripherally or centrally as the discipline suggests.

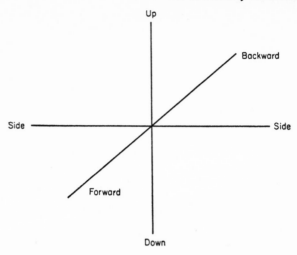

Fig. 6. Axes of movement in personal space.

When locomotion, elevation and turning are added to these *air patterns*, the body produces *floor patterns* as it moves into the general space.

3 DYNAMIC AWARENESS

The *third* group is concerned with the quality of the dance, knowing *'how'* to do *'what'* *'where'*. The intuitive, emotional powers of the dancer are called upon.

Every human movement is linked with an *effort*. This effort is the inner impulse that originates a movement; it gives expression to the action, creating the moods and communicating the inner attitudes and drives of the body. As we express ourselves verbally in sentences composed of words or phrases, so we can express non-verbally in movement sentences and phrases containing many degrees of effort. Effort may be analysed into the four basic factors of time, weight, space and flow and each of these factors sub-divides into two basic and contrasting elements.

TIME	*Sudden*	– the ability of the mover to respond immediately.
	Sustained	– the ability to allow movement to continue for a long time.
WEIGHT	*Firm*	– the ability to exert muscular resistance.
	Fine touch	– the ability to use minimal muscular exertion.

SPACE
┌──────Direct   – the ability to move in an economical unilateral way.
└──────Flexible – the ability to move in an extravagant multilateral way.

FLOW
┌──────Bound – the ability to stop movements at any time.
└──────Free – the ability to allow movements to stream out with ease, the ability to stop being almost absent.

Effort Actions

There are eight basic effort actions and all movement contains them or variations of them. Every effort action can be felt or experienced with the whole or part of the body participating. The effort actions are built up through different combinations of the effort elements (Figure 7).

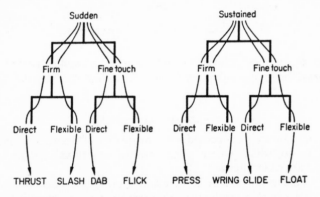

Fig. 7. Diagram showing the build-up of effort actions from combinations of effort elements.

Effort can be taught in many ways:

1 Through the use of action words which stimulate movements of a contrasting nature, for example quick and slow, light and heavy, smooth and jerky.
2 Percussion instruments with their various qualities of sound can stimulate and accompany the training of effort actions.
3 Rhythm is closely linked with effort and a metrical rhythm containing contrasts of time, weight and space can establish a movement phrase with the same qualities.
4 Natural rhythms taken from nature can be used as stimuli to teach efforts; for example the sea, stormy or calm; the wind; volcanic eruption.

These three groups – *Body Awareness, Spatial Awareness, Dynamic Awareness* – cover the basic language and thus provide the material of dance.

To get the maximum educational value from this material, appropriate selection must be made suitable to the age, ability and previous experience of the children. Here we can make use of Laban's comprehensive research into the organization of human movement. He arranged sixteen basic movement themes in a logical and scientific order. They progress parallel to the normal physical and mental growth and development of the child.

THE SIXTEEN BASIC MOVEMENT THEMES

1 *Body Awareness (5 to 6 years)*

   (i)   The body as a unit in motion and stillness,

   (ii)   Symmetric and asymmetric use of the body,

   (iii) Emphasis on parts of the body,

   (iv) Leading the movement with specific parts of the body,

   (v)   Weight transference and gesture,

   (vi) Parts of the body in contact.

2 *The Awareness of Weight and Time (5 to 8 years)*

   (i)   Weight qualities,

   (ii)   Time qualities,

   (iii) Weight-time qualities,

   (iv) Metre,

   (v)   Rhythm.

3 *The Awareness of Space (6 to 8 years)*

   (i)   Using the space,

   (ii)   Spatial areas,

   (iii) Body zones,

   (iv) Extensions in space,

   (v)   Space words,

   (vi) Basic spatial actions.

4 *The Awareness of the Flow of Weight of Body in Space and Time (7 to 9 years)*

   (i)   Successive and simultaneous body flow,

   (ii)   Free flow and bound flow qualities,

    (iii) Flexible and direct space qualities,

    (iv) Flow-space qualities,

    (v) Flow-time qualities,

    (vi) Flow-weight qualities,

    (vii) Weight-space qualities,

    (viii) Space-time qualities,

    (ix) Phrasing and punctuation.

5 *Adaptation to a Partner (8 to 11 years)*

    (i) Doing the same,

    (ii) Conversations in movement,

    (iii) Dancing together.

6 *The Instrumental Use of the Body (8 to 11 years)*

    (i) The meaning of the instrumental use,

    (ii) The basic body actions and stillness,

    (iii) Combinations of the body actions,

    (iv) Sequences of actions.

7 *The Awareness of Basic Effort Actions (9 to 11 years)*

    (i) Thrusting and slashing,

    (ii) Floating and gliding,

    (iii) Wringing and pressing,

    (iv) Flicking and dabbing,

    (v) Compensatory efforts,

    (vi) Efforts through basic body actions,

    (vii) Efforts through various parts of body,

    (viii) Effort through music.

8 *Occupational Rhythms (10 to 13 years)*

    (i) Miming working actions,

    (ii) Work in pairs or groups,

    (iii) The rhythm of action: 3 parts – preparation, action, recovery,

    (iv) Moods and working actions,

    (v) Work dances.

9 *The Awareness of Shape in Movement (10 to 13 years)*

    (i) Basic space patterns,

    (ii)   Floor patterns and air patterns,

    (iii) The size of the movement,

    (iv) Body shape.

10 *Transitions Between the Basic Effort Actions (11 to 14 years)*
    (i)   Gradual change,
    (ii) Less gradual changes,
    (iii) Abrupt changes.

11 *Orientation in Space (12 to 16 years)*
    (i)   Establishing the dimensional cross,
    (ii) Establishing the diagonal cross,
    (iii) Establishing the three planes.

12 *The Combination of Shapes and Efforts (13 to 16 years)*
    (i)   Giving effort and form (shape),
    (ii) Colouring the form (accent-speed),
    (iii) Efforts and orientation (effort-cube),
    (iv) Moving with free use of effort, shape and orientation.

13 *Elevation (14 to 16 years)*
    (i)   Getting away from the floor,
    (ii) Parts of the body taking weight up into the air,
    (iii) Shapes and elevation,
    (iv) Effort and elevation,
    (v) Landing,
    (vi) Elevation without jumping,
    (vii) Partner and group play,
    (viii) Music and elevation.

14 *The Awakening of Group Feeling (15 to 18 years)*
    (i)   Leading and adapting,
    (ii) Mimetic group action,
    (iii) Time relationships,
    (iv) Space relationships,
    (v) Weight relationships,
    (vi) Flow relationships.

15 *Group Formations* (*16 to 18 years*)

   (i)   Group acting as a unit,

   (ii)   Linear group formations,

   (iii) Solid group formations,

   (iv) Irregular group formations,

   (v)   Visual aids for formations,

   (vi) Group formations arising out of improvisation.

16 *The Expressive Qualities of Movement* (*16 to 18 years*)

   (i)   Content of a dance composition,

   (ii)   Choreographic forms,

   (iii) The expressive quality or moods of movement.

Using the Themes. From the graph (Figure 8) it can be seen that permutations of themes 1–4 form the matrix of lessons planned for the 5 to 7-year-olds, themes 2–10 for 9 to 11 years.

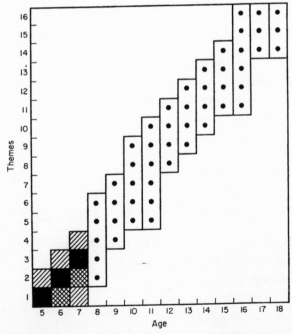

Fig. 8. Graph showing the progression of the sixteen movement themes for ages 5 to 18 years.

The teacher may build a lesson around a movement theme, keeping to pure movement ideas without resorting to additional stimuli. Indeed, the warming and limbering and the movement training sections of the lesson plan are usually more successful if this is done. The climax of the lesson can then be enriched with the introduction of additional imaginative ideas.

STIMULI IN DANCE

These can be classified into four groups:

1 Aural stimuli, from sounds via the ears, including:
   (a) mouth sounds,
   (b) body sounds,
   (c) verbal tasks,
   (d) percussion,
   (e) music – instrumental, recorded and taped.

2 Visual stimulation, observing through the eyes such things as:
   (a) the movement of other children or the teacher,
   (b) television, films, theatre,
   (c) paintings, sculpture, architecture,
   (d) natural sources of power – e.g. sea and wind,
   (e) mechanical sources of power – e.g. machinery.

3 Tactile stimulation, appreciating through the sense of touch:
   (a) the flexibility of, for example, a length of rope,
   (b) the rigidity of a structure,
   (c) the plasticity, the malleable or sticky nature of a substance,
   (d) the smoothness, roughness, sharpness, spikiness of a surface.

4 Literary stimulation, originating a movement idea, symbolic of the original concept, through hearing or reading some story, poem or prose in, for instance:
   (a) a newspaper,
   (b) historical records,
   (c) biblical sources,
   (d) mythology,
   (e) fiction.

In dance we are no longer concerned with teaching set movement patterns, except for demonstration work, but rather with self-expression. This does not mean 'please yourself', but rather the ability to express chosen movement themes in an individual way. Thus, the themes are chosen by the teacher, as the basis of the lesson plan, to give the class opportunities to learn the language of dance through

exploring the spelling and grammar; how to make sentences in movement and how to communicate ideas and tell stories.
The format of the lesson plan follows that suggested in Chapter 4.

1 Warming and limbering,
2 Movement training,
3 Climax,
4 Unwinding.

A Typical Lesson for 5 to 7-year-olds

The work will be extremely simple with plenty of locomotion and a great deal of contrast and repetition to give a feeling of security. Accompaniment should be very simple, probably only percussion instruments being used.

Lesson themes: 1 Action – locomotion and stillness,
2 Space – high and low,
3 Quality – quick and slow.

Relationships: 5-year-olds with the teacher only,
6 to 7-year-olds progress to work in twos.

	Limitations	*Possible coaching*
WARMING AND LIMBERING	(a) Moving and stopping. Repeat at least 3 times before giving coaching points.	Encourage use of general space – different directions. Immediate response to stop! Simple rhythmic repetitive phrase.
	(b) Standing – working on spot in own space showing high and low positions.	Rising and falling – encourage variations in tempo, e.g. slow rise, quick fall.
	(c) Return to (a) and add (b) so that a sequence is developed moving and stop in a high or a low position, hold, then change to opposite level and hold, return to original level and hold. Repeat sequence a number of times.	Vary speeds of rising and falling.
MOVEMENT TRAINING	(a) Own choice of starting position, either high or low – rising and falling with hands leading. Try elbows leading.	With 5-year-olds all begin at same level.
	(b) Return to moving and stopping with stress on levels and speed. Try low and slow, contrasted with high and quick.	Use words to get slow quality (stealthy), heaviness (creep, crawl). High quick should involve light jumps and soft footwork.

	Limitations (cont.)	Possible coaching (cont.)
CLIMAX	(a) Moving quickly, jump and stop (high) 3 times.	5 to 6-year-olds – free use of space.
	(b) Sink slowly to low shape and move slowly close to floor.	6 to 7-year-olds – focus on centre of room – closing in with (a), on the spot and
	(c) Rise slowly, sink quickly 3 times.	opening out with (b), on the spot with (c) and (d).
	(d) Rise slowly ready to repeat from (a).	
UNWIND	Finish quietly.	

A Typical Lesson for 7 to 9-year-olds

The work is still simple, with plenty of repetition and coaching, plenty of activity and lots of elevation. Develop the rhythmic quality.

Lesson themes: 1 Action – elevation and turning
  2 Space – directions
  3 Quality – sudden/firm/light
      sustained/firm/light

Relationships: Working in twos and threes.

	Limitations	Possible coaching
WARMING AND LIMBERING	(a) Moving freely to rhythmic accompaniment.	Simple repetitive rhythm. Encourage different directions and levels. Try different speeds.
	(b) Moving freely, introduce turns and stop in a shape.	Shape related to directions: high, low, wide, narrow, forward, backward.
	(c) Moving freely with turns and jumps.	Encourage variety in shape and level of jumps.
	(d) Develop a sequence, e.g. move (count 1 to 3), leap, stop, hold and hold.	
MOVEMENT TRAINING	(a) Check on body shapes in a held position to get variety. Concentrate on stretched shapes contrasted with curled up shapes.	Different levels and basically reaching into different directions. Opening and closing with different parts leading.
	(b) Moving and jumping and land curling up slowly then stretching out quickly. Try move, jump and land, curl up quickly, stretch slowly. Different combinations of time and weight.	Encourage 'accent' in movement. Body parts leading in different directions and at different levels.
CLIMAX	Working in twos – have a starting position.	Different relationships.

Limitations (cont.)	*Possible coaching (cont.)*
Sequence:	
(a) Curled up together – slowly rise.	Variety of parts leading.
(b) Move away suddenly, travel and leap and stop in own choice of shape and hold.	Sudden, firm quality.
(c) Turn slowly and return slowly to partner, encircle and drop quickly to original starting position ready to repeat.	Choose own weight element. Own spontaneous accompaniment of body/mouth sounds to develop.
UNWIND Finish quietly.	

A Typical Lesson for 9 to 11-year-olds

Encourage simplicity and clarity, insist on quality and plenty of action.

Lesson themes: 1 Action – body shapes,
2 Space – floor and air patterns,
3 Quality – flexible and direct.

Relationships: Small groups.

	Limitations	*Possible coaching*
WARMING AND LIMBERING	(a) Move freely making curved floor patterns. Change to angular floor patterns.	Clarity of pattern – idea reflected in total body shape and attitude.
	(b) Develop a sequence contrasting curved and angular floor patterns.	
	(c) Trace curved patterns in air with various body parts – change to angular air patterns.	Good use of space – near and far.
	(d) Move freely, either curved or angular air pattern in personal space, change to opposite.	Variety in levels, directions, speed and weight.
MOVEMENT TRAINING	(a) Teach and explore the 4 basic body shapes of arrow, wall, ball and screw.	Move into and out of shapes in direct or flexible manner.
	(b) Starting position – any body shape, move out of it and into another. Repeat these two shapes and produce a repetitive rhythmic sequence.	Progress by adding locomotion at any level.

Limitations (cont.)	*Possible coaching (cont.)*
(c) In twos 'chance choreography', i.e. both perform own sequence together – be aware of moments when a chance relationship occurs. Try to develop this.	Teacher dictates the length of the phrase.
CLIMAX In small groups of 4 or 5. Take 3 shapes+locomotion and prepare a sequence which begins with a group shape and returns to same.	Integration with a movement idea? Action, not talk. Travel together. Get a rhythmic accompaniment for each group, e.g. a piece of percussion.
UNWIND Finish quietly.	

Such a lesson for any age group could well last a number of weeks where the children have one lesson per week. Progression could be through:

(i) consolidation, the whole lesson being repeated with no new material.

(ii) some development of some parts of the previous lesson.

(iii) the introduction of some new material to reinforce the original.

(iv) a change in one theme only so as to alter the bias or flavour of a particular aspect of movement in the group of lesson themes.

The Response from the Primary Children

Girls are usually general in response, enjoying the action of dance but also appreciating the quieter moments. The boys respond well to dramatic work and are particularly inventive as top juniors when given percussion or words as stimuli. The content of the work must always be geared to the boys, the aim being to avoid purposeless, effeminate movements.

What to Dance about with Top Juniors and Secondary Classes

Abstract movement themes provide the 'material' of dance and the 'texture' can be influenced by extra stimuli, beginning with variety in inflexion and tone in the teacher's voice which can invoke different qualities in movement and may produce a dramatic situation. The 'feeling' of the physical experience suggests an idea of 'moving like a——' and this concrete imagery feeds back into the physical performance and enhances it.

Movement is life, and dance, being at the very heart of life, is very easily integrated with any topic or subject. The chosen topic or subject should be broken down and translated into movement themes and these can be taught as usual in the warming and limbering and

H

movement training sections of the lesson. The extra stimulus derived from the topic or subject is then introduced in the climax which will communicate the idea through movement which contains the quality and clarity of the previous training.

Movement ideas can be taken from various sources – life, nature or fantasy.

1 Seasonal dances:

    (a) The four seasons;
    (b) Snow, rain, wind, ice, frost;
    (c) Planting, reaping, harvest;
    (d) Hallowe'en, Christmas, Easter, Guy Fawkes.

2 Magical dances:

    (a) Spells and witchcraft;
    (b) Masks.

3 Ritual dances:

    (a) Animal hunting;
    (b) War and peace;
    (c) Marriage, birth and death.

4 Topical dances:

    (a) The environment, e.g. the circus, the fair;
    (b) Newspapers, radio, television, e.g. landing on the moon.

5 Historical, Biblical and literary:

    (a) Myths, legends and stories;
    (b) Prose and poetry.

6 Mathematical and architectural:

    (a) Shape;
    (b) Size and dimension.

7 Scientific:

    (a) Changing forms;
    (b) Space travel.

8 Occupational:

    (a) Agriculture;
    (b) Machines.

9 Other forms of dance:

    (a) Folk;

(b) Ballet.

10 Other physical activities:
   (a) Swimming;
   (b) Athletics;
   (c) Games;
   (d) Drama.

Dance Drama

The easiest and quickest way to find something to dance about is to take a story and be expressive about it. This usually turns out to be mime and not dance. To prevent this happening the movement characteristics arising from the story must be expressed in the language of dance. Results in dance drama very soon become purposeless if the ideas cannot be adequately expressed in movement. Experience in pure dance is therefore essential to progress and satisfaction in this aspect of creative movement.

Dance drama is based upon relationships and involves contrast or conflict. A dramatic relationship develops naturally and more easily between conflicting spatial and effort characteristics.

Accompaniment in dance is essential and should be present for the major part of any lesson. Only occasionally in a lesson will the class work in silence and, usually, only when the work is such that a common rhythm or length of phrase is impossible or could influence or detract from the movement being developed.

As a rule accompaniment is simple and supports the movement in quality and form. Percussion, particularly the tunable tambour and beater, is invaluable if used with variety and sensitivity.

The spoken word, mouth sounds and body sounds can be very effective if used discriminately.

Music, either recorded or taped, can include solo instrumental and orchestral extracts, but the live pianist proves the most satisfactory form of accompaniment. This is especially true if the pianist can improvise as well as sight read so that the music and the movement are created together.

In any one lesson a balance of different types of accompaniment should be the aim.

The Effects of a Well-taught Programme of Dance

1 It preserves or rekindles the natural desire to enjoy movement for movement's sake.
2 It trains control of the body and develops an understanding of its powers and limitations.

3 The dance develops poise and gives confidence in self through increased mobility, stamina and body awareness.

4 Children are made aware of dance as an art form, a living, changing, transient art form which can reinforce other creative arts.

5 Relationships are highlighted, co-operation is developed in creative work which could overflow into, and lead to improvement in, behaviour and manners.

6 It gives the child an appreciation of music through intelligent listening to the accompaniment.

Chapter 13

Further Considerations of Teaching Technique –
'Process and Product' in Physical Education –
The Teacher's Rôle – Presentation of Work –
Discipline – Observation – Demonstrations –
Movement Quality and Standard of Work –
Progression – Accidents – Exemption – Posture

PROCESS AND PRODUCT

In all branches of education it is essential that the teacher should differentiate between experiences and the results of those experiences. There is the dangerous tendency to assess the activities of any class solely by the tangible results of their work in, for example, craft. No judgement can be made from the product alone. The process must also be considered. It is the lived experience that contributes to the child's development.

The value of an activity must be measured in terms of the child's effort, of his growth in control and self-reliance and his joy of accomplishment, not merely by the extent to which the results approximate to adult standards. The teacher must certainly be clear for himself of the relative value of 'process' and 'product' in physical education. For instance, too great a stress on 'product' in games leads to the coaching of a team at the expense of the majority of average players.

There is no doubt that, for children, 'process' in physical education is quite as valuable as 'product'. It is, however, less showy from the teacher's point of view. Nevertheless, no teacher of integrity will put material results first. Physical education has benefits for all children and adolescents and the benefits are gained by doing, by making mistakes and by overcoming them, with emphasis on the process as well as on the result.

The consideration of the result has a limited but definite value, namely that it may set a standard towards which to strive. Such standards will, of course, vary with the age of the children and the teacher will learn to gauge them both by observation and by taking part himself in gymnastics, dance, games, swimming and athletic activities.

The Child's Purpose or Incentive

The teacher's purpose and goal in physical education have been stressed but the child's purposes must also be considered. A teacher of adults enlists the co-operation of his students by revealing to them his own aims and purpose. The teacher of children can only secure the maximum co-operation of the class by providing some incentive for activity which suits their stage of development. In the physical education lessons the teacher does not make such appeals as 'If you don't do this you will never move well', but draws on 'the children's instinctive activities and interests, such as their natural delight in running and jumping, climbing and swinging on apparatus, competing against self and others.

The mental appeal of physical education tends to develop from the concrete to the abstract. Younger children like to have something definite and concrete to aim for, and the achievement of that aim or standard becomes an end in itself. Thus a continuous practice of landing deeply, using only the floor, has a clear aim for the young child in the depth and resilience achieved.

Secondary school work, of less definite and more abstract appeal, requires very clear teaching, for it is the limitations set by the teacher that make the class feel progress to justify their effort.

Thus the most effective teacher is the one who not only is clear as to the adult purpose of the work in hand, safe landings from heights on apparatus developing from the practice just cited, but also provides a purpose or incentive which the children can understand and appreciate.

THE TEACHER'S RÔLE

Teaching technique was briefly considered in Chapter 2, but presentation of work has also been implicit in the consequent discussion of material. Thus the reader will, by this time, have a better idea of the teacher's rôle as being one of unobtrusive control, albeit ensuring that the whole class is working with enjoyment and purpose. The good teacher guides and leads his class to discover ways of moving and developing skills for themselves; he sets standards; helps the children to appreciate what is 'good' performance; puts them on their mettle to do the best work of which they are individually capable. There is a tendency in teaching today to omit this practice of giving the children incentive to strive, to respond to challenge, to gain satisfaction from effort. It is vital to learning to encourage each child to vie in this way with himself and it should involve him in both doing and thinking. The teacher, too, should be completely involved, for if he merely gives the tasks and leaves the children to their learning they will only dabble in the process. He should present his work with such obvious enthusiasm that every child in the class catches the feeling and is aware of the teacher's personal interest.

PRESENTATION OF WORK

As the immediate aim is to get the children moving, *tasks* should be simply and economically worded. Some teachers try vainly by wearying repetition to eliminate faults before they occur. If, however, the work is new and properly selected for the particular class, the children ought to have to learn by trial and a certain amount of error, that is by overcoming difficulties and correcting their own mistakes, so that they feel their own growing ability. The teacher should be positive in his guidance and avoid suggesting faults and difficulties before they happen.

As a general principle, the teacher should always create a need for an explanation before giving it. This means that in all aspects of physical education the performers start by doing something actively – let the class have an informal 'go' at the work – and, when they have experienced the problems, they will be interested in the teacher's suggestions or in watching others demonstrate.

It should always be possible to suggest some fresh challenge before repeating any activity. To do so gives purpose and interest, whereas to repeat for no reason may indicate that the class is filling in time because the teacher is at a loss how to proceed.

Voice

The contact between teacher and children is vitally important to the success of the lesson and is largely dependent on the most obvious means of communication: the teacher's voice. Whilst a level of working noise in the class is acceptable, too much chattering dispels concentration and it has already been stated that the children should be thinking as well as doing. Quality in the teacher's voice is most essential to grip the children's attention and stimulate the proper response; on the other hand both shouting and pitching the voice too high cause excitement: it is true to say that a 'noisy teacher makes a noisy class'.

Coaching

The lesson, however, is meant for child activity, and *not* for teacher talking, so having briefly, clearly and simply given the task to get the activity started, the teacher may, after observation, see the need to coach, though coaching should not anticipate what the children may be able to find out for themselves. Coaching should be given *as the class works*, giving *one* understood point based on close observation and to do specifically with the task. In this way the children are helped to achieve *clarity* in their work.

The inexperienced or poor teacher breeds inaccurate and confused work in a class by not helping, or even allowing, the children to confine their thoughts to the limitations of the task. For example, having challenged them to 'Travel about the space in different ways on the feet', he immediately rushes in with coaching points such as 'Remember to use different levels', 'Try a change of speed', 'What about directions?' Meanwhile the variety of ways of travelling on the feet is neglected as the children attempt to keep up with the teacher's fresh demands.

Coaching, then, should not confuse the issue but should help the children to channel their attempts within the limitations currently imposed. It can be immensely encouraging to the teacher to see that, while concentrating on the task in hand, *some* children can demonstrate previous learning and understanding by including incidentally other ideas such as levels, speed changes, directions, etc., but this should not be demanded of the class as a whole if we appreciate their different abilities.

This same point is important in connection with teaching to a *theme*: the aspect of movement being explored at depth cannot of course exist in isolation; other elements of the movement principles will be present but subordinate to the main idea. Thus, movement on a theme of twisting and turning will involve the moving body in use of speed, space, tension and control, but the child must be permitted and helped to concentrate on the desired learning. For him the present experience is enough; he lacks the ability and background to appreciate at once, as his teacher does, the whole scope of the movement factors.

Physical Presence

The work produced by the children is influenced by the teacher's personal appearance, posture, positioning and purposeful movement about the space. When the children stop to listen, the teacher should stand outside the group, where he can see and be seen by every child, *and* he should keep still whilst speaking so as not to divert attention from what he is saying. This keeping still does not preclude gesture, which can often inspire the class by simulating the action to be attempted, but restless pacing to and fro makes it impossible for the children to concentrate on further instructions or explanation. As the children work, however, they should be aware of the teacher moving amongst them, alert and noticing what each one of them is doing. No child should feel able to hide himself away in a corner unobserved by the teacher, nor should any child suffer from having his willing efforts go unnoticed.

DISCIPLINE

The first word and the first activity given in the classroom or cloakroom set the tone of the lesson. If the activity completely involves the children and is demanding enough, the teacher has a grip and it need not go, providing the continuity of the lesson is kept up. *Continuity* of activity or a quick '*follow on*' means that there is no pause between each new task while the teacher obviously thinks what is coming next. Any reasonably skilled and well-prepared teacher is able to think about what comes next while supervising the work the class is actually doing. He is, in effect, carrying two sets of thoughts in his mind, and dividing attention between two consecutive steps in the lesson, but as this is logically developed, memorization should not be difficult. If memory should temporarily fail, the teacher should refer to notes, unobtrusively, while the class works on the previous activity, thus preventing any loss of confidence in his ability. A slow 'follow on' may be due to poor organization, in that apparatus is distributed in a muddled fashion or portable apparatus is wrongly placed and has to be moved twice over. Such arrangements should have been considered as part of the preparation of the lesson.

Thorough preparation, smooth organization, an alert and interested teacher, should result in well-run activity. *Activity* is the best means of discipline; holding the class back can only lead to further disturbance and naughtiness.

It seems that present-day teaching of physical education is quieter and less dominant than hitherto but more effective, for the children are motivated by self-involvement and personal achievement. What they do is done with understanding, what they experience results in active learning.

OBSERVATION

Fundamental to such a rôle is the teacher's ability to observe. This involves him not only in watching what is taking place, but in deliberately trying to understand and feel what he is seeing. For the teacher in the primary school, observation of children, at work and play, is a vital and constant guide to provision, assessment and progress. Observation of movement in physical education lessons is an extension of the classroom opportunities, a revealing and highly-significant source of information. It may, however, impose greater difficulty on the teacher in the secondary school who sees the children only in the movement situation and cannot therefore build up a complete picture of each child. Observation of two kinds has been inferred; general observation of the class as a whole, particular observation of individual children.

Class observation is overt, conscious and with practical intent. It is used to assess:

(i) Class mood, which may be dull, lethargic, lazy, depending on the previous activity or lesson, the weather, the time of day. In this case the teacher uses, or adapts, the prepared introductory activity to inspire and arouse response. On the other hand, the children may arrive in a boisterous, excitable state because of some unusual happening in school or weather conditions such as wind or snow. The activity may allow some outlet for this kind of mood but then impart a quietening effect of concentration and effort.

(ii) Class reaction, which may be uninterested and apathetic to the tasks given. Adaptation may, in this case, be necessary to awaken interest and response.

(iii) Class understanding, which may have failed because the wording of the task has been inaccurate, too difficult or outside the children's previous experience. Rewording, further explanation or regression to a previous stage may be necessary in such cases.

(iv) Class achievement, observation of which requires most skill and discernment, in terms of variety – there may be as many answers as there are children – or sameness, development on previous work. Observation of this kind is the basis of coaching, future provision and demonstration, which will be enlarged upon later. The reader will find it helpful to refer back to Chapter 5 where it was suggested that this type of analytical observation should be based on the three questions: What, How and Where?

Observation of individuals may be of three kinds:

(i) Looking at individuals who are known to be outstanding, so as to know how to help them to progress further; and, possibly more important, noting the *efforts* of those who are not generally out-standing in performance so that they can be encouraged and helped to develop what they are achieving. The latter group may include the timid, the nervous and the lazy; but also the adventurous and the accident-prone who may endanger themselves and others in the class.

(ii) Concentration in a lesson may be on a particular child for the purpose of an individual study. In spite of the importance of such a child study, the observation should be unobtrusive, and should not be at the expense of the rest of the class.

(iii) Notice should be taken of individual well-being in this physical setting when the children are stripped. This may give the teacher evidence that a particular child is not well, is unhappy, unclean, poorly dressed, suffering from some skin infection or bruising; and action can be taken to relieve the condition.

DEMONSTRATIONS

Observation of movement is important to the teacher, but seeing the movement of others is also an important part of the children's education. Once children have passed the nursery and lower infant age-range, they have an increasing interest in other children's performance. The teacher makes use of this interest to intersperse quick, informal demonstrations in his lessons, then helps the children to understand and learn from what they see.

Selection of Those to Demonstrate

This selection depends on the age and experience of the class. It can be progressed, catering first of all for younger children or beginners:

(i) *Half* the class observing the other half, in turn. The group situation hides identity, therefore none of the children are self-conscious or inhibited in their movement. Observation of such a number of performers is difficult but there is great advantage in having every child practise both rôles, performer and observer.

(ii) A *few* children perform while the rest observe, the teacher having selected the performers because each shows a different, worthwhile answer to the challenge or because each has some point in common. Observation of the few is easier but care must be taken not to select always the same two or three children who may be expected to produce outstanding work, as this denies the majority of the class the opportunity to perform; and incidentally the few miss the chance to observe, as well as possibly becoming too cocksure and complacent about their ability. For different purposes, every child must have some contribution worth watching at some time.

(iii) The class arranged in *pairs*, one child performs observed by partner, in turn. As there is only one mover to concentrate on, observation is easy, providing that the teacher gives specific points to look for. The performers move with very little self-consciousness, although attention is focused on them as individuals. The disadvantage of this arrangement is that the teacher cannot check and discuss what each child has observed so that there is no guaranteed standard of work.

(iv) As the children become accustomed to being watched the teacher may select *one* child to perform for the whole class. This method is most suitable when the teacher wishes to show the class a *good* performance though the children should not, as would have been the case in teaching formal gymnastics, be left with the idea that this is *the* way to answer the challenge. Apart from its use in setting a standard, this kind of demonstration may be designed by the teacher to emphasize positively the terms of the task. If a poor answer is required for contrast, for example a heavy landing, the teacher should demonstrate rather than risk destroying such confidence as may be possessed by a poor performer.

(v) *Group* demonstrations can be given after working at a group task – e.g. a group using leaps to make a movement sequence over forms. Demonstrations of group work on apparatus may be used, the children watching being told what the challenge is, and then judging if this has been carried out. This is also a way of showing a new activity added to a group work arrangement. All the class watches so that they will all know what to do on arrival at that group place.

Organization

Before any demonstration, every child must *first* have had the chance of trying out the movement in his own way, so that he has got the feeling of it, and has experienced the difficulties and the challenges.

As he selects, the teacher should try to warn those who are to perform so that they are prepared in every way for the demonstration. This obviates the embarrassing situation of a child, overcome by the sudden request to show his work, evading on the pretext of having forgotten what he did.

The class should next be organized, spaced out so that they can all see the demonstration, maybe sitting on the floor if this helps observation. Those performing need plenty of space to move freely and show their ideas to advantage, so it is important that the others do not crowd round them. Good spacing also enables the teacher to see that every child is involved in the exercise, whether performing or observing. Now the teacher should prepare the observers to watch by giving them *one thing* to look at, e.g. 'Which parts of the body are in contact with the floor?', or 'What pathways are being used?' Unless the children receive this specific guidance they will look without seeing *and* the teacher will also find the subsequent discussion difficult to steer; in fact it may develop along the lines of 'Did anybody see anything interesting happening?' to which there could be forty valid answers. The one thing to look for could be 'Are they (is he) answering the challenge?', an important question. If the answer is 'Yes', and the children should be able to support their assertion, the teacher may use the opportunity to re-emphasize the limitations imposed. The answer should not be negative if the teacher's own observation is keen, but if this should happen, the situation needs careful and tactful handling, lest confidence and trust between performer and teacher are broken. This can be resolved if the teacher helps the class to appreciate the good points in the demonstration, whilst helpfully suggesting improvements.

After the demonstration the teacher should:

1 Conduct a quick, precise discussion based on the question asked, ensuring that the children have not only 'seen' (physically) what is considered good but can understand and reason out why and how it is good.
2 Thank and praise the performer(s) and draw out from the class some helpful comments and advice for an even better standard so that he (they) also learns from the demonstration.
3 Allow the whole class to have another turn so as to reinforce their new understanding and allow new ideas to emerge whilst fresh in the mind. This is a very important point to remember, especially for those who performed and wish to apply the advice they were given. It is also important to the teacher for it gives him time to observe the fresh attempts and thus assess the value of the observation and his own handling of the discussion that followed.

Value

Teaching by demonstration is of value if it gives the class a clear idea of the aim of the activity. It must be quick so that it does not hold up the class's activity any longer than necessary. With this proviso, a demonstration may be better understood by the class than are verbal suggestions only. The children benefit from seeing so many different, and possibly new, variations in one challenge and this increases their own vocabulary and ideas. Most children like being chosen to show work and this may motivate them to greater effort and inventiveness. The work shown, provided that the teacher's own observation is good, establishes a standard of movement, good and pleasing to look at, for each child to aim for, and this too increases the effort put into the activity. The discussion with the teacher increases movement understanding and creates confidence as the children appreciate that they are on the right lines. Vagueness in their own work may be clarified as they see others producing clearer answers. Also, as they observe the efforts of others, the children appreciate qualities in movement different from theirs and become more keenly aware of their own personal movement characteristics. They become increasingly able to help and criticize each other constructively, more interested in each other and in the work. This increasing awareness makes them more alert to what is going on around them in the hall, gymnasium, playground or field, which results in greater concentration in lessons. So, in partner or group work, when not performing themselves, they watch, offer helpful suggestions, check apparatus, take responsibility and are generally more involved in their physical education, and working together sympathetically.

Disadvantages

If over-used and not purposefully utilized, demonstrations may kill the pace of a lesson for they will be needlessly time-consuming in a situation meant for activity for the whole class. In unskilled hands, performance and discussion tend to go on too long and the teacher should remember to keep both of these short and to the point, and then get the whole class active again. Young and inexperienced children who are exploring their own abilities have little to show and are better getting on with their own activity. This also applies to the more experienced who, when exploring a new theme or sequence, have nothing to show if asked too soon to demonstrate. Of course, like any teaching method, teaching by demonstration should not be used exclusively or too much, for it will then lose impact and effect.

MOVEMENT QUALITY AND STANDARD OF WORK

The teacher must understand, and get over to the class, differences in movement quality brought about by the different use of the factors of speed, space, tension and control. It is the sensitivity to combine these factors, to just the right degree for the activity required, that produces easy, fluent movement.

The teacher gives all-round experience of movement quality by:

(i) his choice of activity and

(ii) his appreciation of individual performance.

It is the teacher who, while praising the natural quality at which each child excels, will aim later at getting the relatively slow child to attempt with some success quick, light work, and the child who prefers direct movement to work at twisting, flexible body movements. The teacher must prevent the work being shallow and in one groove, and inspire a high standard of effort and performance by making the children attempt ways of moving not so natural to them. It can be seen that two courses of action are continually in front of the teacher; (a) to attain a higher standard of work by suggesting limitations, or (b) to get more variety of work through creative activity.

The teacher who is superficial or who fails to perceive high quality of work, will tend to say, too speedily and too often, 'What else can you do?' and little standard of work will be asked. The level of performance will remain shallow. If the work is shallow and superficial, the children will lose interest and incentive. The teacher should never be willing to accept poor work without mention, coaching, and even self-demonstration of such things as landings, footwork, lifting and placing of apparatus. Credit should be given for the effort made, but to over-praise in terms such as 'very good', without specifying how and indicating ways of improving the work further, limits the children's response and their appreciation of standards. The teacher should be constantly stressing such things as the preparedness of the body in the starting position, the exact repetition of the sequence, the clarity of the finishing position.

Teaching by *contrast* is conducive to the development of quality in movement. It will be obvious from the analysis (Figure 1) and the suggestions given in gymnastics and dance schemes that contrasting movements are frequently linked. This is a most effective means of teaching quality in movement, but only if the teacher helps the children to experience the full extent of the two contrasting elements. For example, in curling and stretching, every part curls in towards the centre in strong contrast to stretching from the centre of the body to the limit of the extremities.

PROGRESSION

In all aspects of physical education there must be *progression* and by this is meant the series of changes that an activity undergoes, so that it may gradually become more difficult of performance, stronger in effects, and of steadily increasing interest to the individual. All through school life, the children are growing and developing in physical abilities and mental outlook, and progression fits in with this. A general comparison of the work for primary and secondary children shows that activities and themes are repeated with little, or no apparent, variation and so seem to lack progression. The progression, however, is not one of increased difficulty but increase in the standard asked, and is made by the limitations the teacher sets so that the class produces greater variety, accuracy, effort and quality.

Progression should occur from lesson to lesson, and within the lesson itself, so that the children are constantly pitting themselves against the challenge of the increasingly high standard of achievement set by the teacher.

ACCIDENTS

Accidents should be preventable by the teacher's foresight and control, as well as the children's previous training in response and body management. By no means should the children be made accident-conscious, timid or fussy. It is generally found that if performers progress at their own rate and appreciate the need for co-operation and abiding by the rules, very few accidents do occur. Occasional minor accidents may happen, but the teacher can do much to minimize the effect, especially on confidence, by applying sympathy of a cheerful and robust kind. The ability to stand occasional knocks without showing self-pity is part of the training which should come from the child's physical education. This is not to say that the teacher should be careless of knocks and bruises, but he must learn to judge between slight and more serious injury, and here knowledge of the reactions of individual children will help. Every teacher should have some knowledge of 'first aid', including simple remedies for minor injuries. In the event of what appears to be a serious accident, he should keep calm and discourage indiscriminate sympathy and crowding round by the rest of the class; if possible giving them something to go on with while he himself attends to the injured. Meanwhile a responsible girl or boy can be sent for help so that neither the casualty nor the class suffers neglect.

EXEMPTION FROM PHYSICAL ACTIVITY

The teacher should, by his planning and teaching, ensure that the children prefer to take part and enjoy doing so. No one should wish to opt out for fear of finding himself compelled to attempt something beyond his powers, for the activity is geared to each child's natural ability and standard.

Children who are regularly exempt on medical grounds should be encouraged to help – by steadying apparatus, replacing jumping canes, checking small apparatus – to make them feel useful and involved with the class. If suitably shod, they may even try some activity, for instance in group work where skill may be practised without over-exertion. The teacher should, however, take no risks in allowing to take part any child about whom a doubt exists; the responsibility for deciding is his, on evidence from parent or doctor. Younger children, especially, must be protected from their own enthusiasm.

With adolescent girls, the question of exemption at the *menstrual period* arises. For the average normal girl, taking part in physical education lessons can do nothing but good. The menstrual flow is hurried on and pain from congestion and constipation is dispersed. The teacher can do much to influence the girls to a balanced attitude here. There should not be an expectancy of disability in connection with this most natural function, so long as the girls are taught the hygiene of the period.

POSTURE

In teaching, there is no longer an obvious concern for 'good posture' in terms of checking, with remedial intent, such pathological deviations as kyphosis, lordosis, scoliosis and flat foot. On the other hand, too violent a swing away from this formal approach did result in a stage of careless disregard for the production or benefits of the upright carriage.

Whilst no longer providing specific exercises for class faults of posture, or giving remedial treatment to individuals, the teacher should be aware of the need to cater for the struggle against gravity and the habitual forward inclination of the body in everyday activity. Increasing body awareness and control of body weight, the lift of the head and breast bone experienced in flight, the full extension of the body in stretching, the stress on poise and standing tall at the conclusion of a lesson; these all help to produce in the child a feeling of positive posture in a physical sense.

Physiologically, vigorous exercise and the resulting expansion of the lung cage are vital to the kind of carriage desired. So, too, is the vitality derived by all the body systems from the effects of muscle activity. It would seem necessary, therefore, to have as many opportunities in the school day as possible for children to enjoy such vigorous and massive activity, especially as they are, at the same time, freed from the sedentary occupations which may be encouraging malposture.

But there is more to posture than the physical. Moods, emotions, mental attitudes and states, are all reflected in stance. Few children fail to shake off such conditions when physically active. Thus, it is reasonable to suggest that a balanced programme of physical education could, through the child's successful enjoyment of a widening range of skills, help to produce the desired result of efficient upright posture.

Chapter 14

The Secondary Programme – The Scope –
A Basic Course – Gymnastics – Games Training
(Stages I and II) – Swimming – Dance – Athletics

In recent years several educational reports have stressed the importance of widening the scope of the physical education programme at the secondary stage in preparation for the adult leisure awaiting the girls and boys when they leave school.

'The essential needs in physical education could perhaps be summed up in the words variety, choice, better facilities and links with adult organizations.'

(*Half our Future*, Newsom Report, 1963)

Although in complete agreement with the recommendation, we may feel concern at the way in which it is being implemented in many schools. With no check on previous experience and ability, teachers are offering to 11-year-olds, fresh from the primary schools, a bewildering choice of activities beyond their skill, physique and understanding. The very activities offered depend, for their progress and enjoyment, on a sound range of well-developed skills and, even more important, on basic body management. Such requirements can only derive from a sound course of gymnastics, games training, swimming, dance and athletics; the five areas of physical activity stemming from the child's natural interest and ability. If the child has come from a primary school doing work in these five areas based on an appreciation of the movement principles, one could presumably offer him a widening programme at 11 years of age. But even that would not take into account the immaturity evident in his lack of physique and stamina, and in his inability to make up his mind. If, on the other hand, the child lacks the desired background, the situation is even more premature.

It therefore seems to be absolutely essential that at least the first two, or even three, years in the secondary school should be spent in either (a) providing the basic course which is lacking, or (b) reinforcing what has taken place in the primary school.

This indicates a programme including all five aspects previously mentioned:

1 Gymnastics,
2 Games training,
3 Swimming,
4 Dance,
5 Athletics.

It will be remarked that athletics did not occur in the primary programme – not as a separate entity. However, if the activity suggested in the relevant chapters on gymnastics, games training and dance is considered, it will be obvious that athletic ability has been fostered throughout the primary course. The necessary elements of running, fast and slow; jumping for height and distance; throwing for aim and length; have all been developed, as well as a degree of body control and stamina. With this background, it is easy therefore to introduce athletics as a separate activity at this stage.

Facilities

For such a programme, facilities are naturally more extensive than those provided for a primary school and should help to emphasize the children's sense of promotion by being somewhat different. Depending on the size of the school they should, if possible, include:

1 A fully equipped gymnasium,
2 A field with various pitches for major games, but also providing extra playing areas for practices, minor games and five-a-side versions of the major games,
3 Tennis and netball courts,
4 A sports hall or covered area for wet weather play,
5 A hall or studio with floor suitable for barefoot work in dance,
6 A learner pool or traditional swimming bath, or liberal access to the public baths.

Teaching staff at this stage may be mainly specialist-trained in physical education. There is therefore no intention of discussing and suggesting, in detail, material for the five aspects of the programme. Assuming that the department is run by a specialist, he will prepare syllabuses of work and give advice on their implementation to those teachers, not specially trained, who assist with the subject. It may be of help, however, to indicate the organization and immediate progression of the five aspects to cover a basic course of two years for the children from 11 to 13 years of age. This will also, under re-organization, coincide with the two years (11 to 13) at the top of a middle school, where the work may well be the responsibility of a class teacher.

Segregation

It was deemed neither desirable nor necessary to separate the girls and boys in the primary school for physical education; they were similar in physique and interests, and any differences they showed in skill were mutually beneficial. By this time, however, differences of interest and aptitude are developing and it is usual to segregate and teach the two sexes separately. The five activities listed earlier are certainly suitable for both sexes in the age range under consideration. It is assumed that gymnastics, dance, games training and swimming have all been well taught during the children's primary education. If this is so, then the 11-year-olds will be eager to continue with them all, and will be keenly interested in the addition of athletics to the programme. Teachers may, however, wish to give a different emphasis to the work suggested under the five headings, depending on whether they plan for a class of girls or boys.

Timetable

A daily lesson of physical education is more than ever important for this age group. For the 11-year-old, academic work has quite suddenly become more demanding; an increasing amount of home-work occupies his evenings and he has therefore less time for his favourite energetic evening activities out of doors. He may be growing, thus making increased demands on metabolism to the detriment of stamina; and even 'outgrowing his strength' which may be producing postural problems. So his regular, organized physical education is vital, the emphasis being on its regularity. This means that a double period of games, for instance, on one day can scarcely compensate for another day without any form of physical education on the timetable. There can be no convincing argument against the greater value of two separate single periods as compared with only one 'go' in a double period. Apart from denying the children an opportunity to make a fresh start at the same, or another form, of physical activity on another day, the length of a double period exceeds their physical effort, stamina and, in some cases, interest. The only justification seems to lie in allowing time to travel to a distant playing field or swimming bath.

A BASIC COURSE

Programme

To include all five aspects of activity, a winter and summer programme can be arranged, based on five periods per week:

Winter	*Summer*
2 gymnastics	2 athletics
1 dance	2 games training
1 games training	1 swimming
1 swimming	

The greater emphasis on athletics and games training in the summer term takes full advantage of the finer weather. It also ensures that those children more athletically inclined have full scope for their talent in that one term, whilst those keener on dance or gymnastics benefit more in the autumn and spring terms.

Approach

About six weeks before starting secondary education, the child was leaving the primary school. In the short holiday period there has been no transformation; he is not essentially different in appearance, ability, skill, interest and reaction. He is still light and agile; has boundless energy and enthusiasm; enjoys climbing, jumping and throwing. Most important of all, he is still in the process of acquiring skill; so he should not be asked immediately to apply what skill he has to situations beyond his experience and ability, e.g. quantities of fresh apparatus both larger and higher than in his primary school; games situations complicated by large teams, many rules, full pitches; the deep end and the diving boards at the swimming baths; the intricacies of step and formation in traditional dances; adult standards and equipment on the athletics field.

Ways of Learning

As a child in the primary school he wanted, and was allowed, to explore and experiment in physical education as in other aspects of education. For the moment this is still an appropriate way of learning for him, but the teacher must be observant, watching for signs which will indicate a growing need for adult guidance and support. By the end of the first year in the secondary school a general level of body control and co-ordination has been reached, and the work in physical education may begin to show lack of purpose and clarity, if experiment and exploration continue without direction. Mere exposure to a learning situation is not enough, the children need:

(i) some direct teaching:

e.g. 'Place your hands on the floor directly under your shoulders, fingers together and pointing forward, so that the arms can take your body weight' (Inverted balance on hands).

(ii) some direction in their thinking:

e.g. 'This is one way of getting along the form using hands and feet. See how many more ways you can find' (Child or teacher demonstration).

Changing Needs

In discussion of the primary stage, the activity, particularly in games training and swimming, was justified in terms of fulfilling the child's present needs of enjoyment and skill. It becomes necessary to be rather more objective in planning the physical education of the secondary child. Parents and society are forcing a grown-up rôle on children earlier and earlier. They travel short distances to school by car or bus; go for a drive with parents at the week-end; watch the football match on Saturday afternoon or else see it on television later; listen to pop records; are members of a cinema club. These sophisticated occupations are no substitute, in terms of activity, for the pastimes of a previous generation which cycled, kicked a ball about, climbed trees, skipped, played hopscotch; went swimming, fishing, camping; roller skated. Added to which the modern way of life, with its gadgets, no longer makes it necessary even to do such jobs about the house as stick-chopping. Less and less physical demands are made on the whole body; even the feet have less to do; we can survive by merely using the skills developed in our hands. All these modern trends deprive the child at this age of what is still an inborn urge, the need to be active.

Another change that is being forced upon the girl or boy, in terms of physical inactivity, occurs in the classroom. Much of the learning in the primary school was brought about, or accompanied by, freedom to move about the classroom, the corridor and even further afield. More and more in the secondary school, the child accepts the discipline of sitting at a desk; so movement becomes less and less a constant part of his school day. This indicates that, from the very first approach, the physical education lesson must be stimulating and interesting, providing both mental and physical challenge. As a junior, always on the move, he reacted in physical education from sheer joy and exuberance; now in the secondary school, the child needs to appreciate the purpose of the activity he is being asked to take part in. It must inspire and urge him to move by its relevance; by the challenge it makes on his physical skill and prowess, on his mental alertness, his sense of adventure, his fearlessness. Even more so than in the primary school, it is important that lessons are not looked upon just as a means of 'letting off steam'. This is not to say that lessons should not be lively and full of fun; they most certainly should; but they should also be challenging to the children, both physically and mentally.

Adaptation to Changing Needs

This can be summarized as follows:

1 Gradual introduction of apparatus, facilities, new activities, advanced rules and organization.

2 Exploration and experiment should no longer be used exclusively but should give way gradually to the challenge of more advanced skills as a result of direction in teaching and thinking.

3 Planning should be more objective so that the movement experience can help to counteract the modern trend by laying particular emphasis on the use of the whole body.

4 Increased stimuli and interest should produce greater purpose in the work so as to stir the child to move, for he no longer has so many opportunities to do so spontaneously and freely, and may not wish to in case he displays social ineptness.

GYMNASTICS

This aspect of physical education continues to be essential to basic skill and body management, particularly at this age, which may be the beginning, or the anticipation, of the adolescent spurt of growth. As suggested earlier, two lessons per week may be set aside in the autumn and spring terms for gymnastics. Included in the 40 or 45 minutes allowed for each lesson, time should be given for completely changing into suitable attire, shorts and vest or leotard for the girls, and showering. The practical health education involved is most essential at this stage of growing-up. This may leave only about 35 minutes teaching time, but with good preparation and organization, and quick 'follow-on' of activity, it should be possible to give the children a full and satisfying lesson.

There are several *new* things to consider in planning the work at this point. The children, if they are commencing at a new school, may have come from several different primary schools, thus they are not only strange to one another but have different backgrounds in physical education, as in everything else. The teacher is new to the children, just as they are new and unknown to him, and it may not be possible to check the gymnastic backgrounds of all, especially if several primary schools are involved. The situation of fully-equipped gymnasium with bigger, and different, fixed and portable apparatus, is also new to the children and may, in fact, be rather alarming.

The teacher therefore needs first to check, by recapitulation or actual development, the basic theme: *Learning to receive weight:* to ensure safety and confidence in the new environment.

Introductory Scheme of Work

The scheme, possibly for the first term, may be based on a main theme of *learning to receive weight* with subordinate themes of *whole body*: shape, using space, curling and stretching, twisting and turning; *parts of the body:* hands and feet working close together or far apart, work on the hands alone; *flow:* travelling and stopping (freeze), sequences on locomotion, free flow in sliding and diving.

The work on flow is very important at this stage for it establishes the *control* which is essential in gymnastics.

It is not necessary to give detailed suggestions for tasks in these themes, as such detail is given in the earlier chapters on gymnastics, but it must be stressed that the different age group involves the teacher in suitable presentation and the claiming of appropriate standards of work. This point was discussed in Chapter 13.

The lesson plan should follow the same development as that used in the primary school.

1 Introduction

(a) *Free Practice*

As the children are more responsible, the limbering activity may become more and more at their choice. They should be encouraged to develop the habit of beginning to work at once on entering the gymnasium. Whole body, as well as feet, needs to be limbered, the movement building up from work on the spot and then travelling. As they warm and feel the suppling effect of the movement, the spine should be involved, not only in curling, stretching and twisting, but also in arching backwards.

(b) *Introductory Activity*

Here the teacher introduces the theme of the lesson and in the first weeks with the new class checks, as with the younger children, their ability to use the space well and respond to his voice.

2 Floor Training

(a) *Work for the Whole Body*

As part of the main theme of receiving weight, work for the whole body will be basically concerned with putting it down softly on to a part, which parts are in contact with the floor during a roll, variety of rolls, rocking from one part to an adjacent part, the shape of the body in rolling and rocking.

(b) *Work for the Legs*

Work for the legs is central to the main theme of receiving weight. The five basic jumps can be used to give experience in take-off preparatory to:

(i) *arriving*, with control, to stay.

(ii) *alighting*, that is using an intermediary contact then taking the body on.

(iii) *landing*, either with the body weight taken low and developing a recovery movement on the hands, or, meeting the ground in a variety of ways and continuing on until the movement dies away.

All of these should be explored on the floor using one or two feet and then developed on to, and from, low apparatus such as mats, forms, spring board, low beams, ropes and wallbars; with further progressions possible using the higher apparatus eventually.

(c) *Weight on the Hands*

The work here is also important to the main theme as weight may be received on the hands in a variety of ways. Experience should be given through tasks using the floor, forms, wallbars, beams, ropes. Feet should assist the hands at first until the children have gained experience, especially of the inverted position.

3 Climax

All the activity suggested in the lesson plan so far prepares for work on apparatus in a group situation, but it may be simpler at first, and time-saving, to organize the climax on a class activity basis. This also gives the teacher the opportunity, in getting out the same apparatus with the whole class, to train the children in its proper care and handling. This training and the progression from class activities to group work will be dealt with later. Details about the class activity method should be looked up in Chapter 6.

4 Conclusion

A quietening movement should end the lesson. The children should leave the gymnasium with a class feeling and an air of poise and relaxation.

The Building up of Group Work in Secondary Gymnastics

Group practices on gymnastics apparatus should occupy at least half of the lesson period. If children have not worked in a fitted gymnasium before, they need to get used to the apparatus and not attempt to use all kinds immediately. Group work at any stage may be built up from class activities, but in a gymnasium where portable and eventually fixed apparatus is to be used, progressive building up of activities is most necessary. The suggestions made here depend on what apparatus is available and must be modified to this.

1 To start with, each group could have a large mat and be encouraged to *approach from all directions* to roll over it and continue on. Different body parts are stressed; so is the ability to move with continuity from one part to another. Different body shapes emerge, e.g. some children roll sideways, some forwards or backwards, others obliquely by putting a shoulder down. These may be developed by encouraging, for example, a roll showing two shapes on the mat smoothly without any pause.

One important outcome of this work should be that the children, right from the start, appreciate a mat as a piece of apparatus to use. It is unfortunate that the latest D.E.S. publication on Safety in Schools has omitted the advice given in Ministry of Education Pamphlet No. 13, *viz.:* 'The use of mats of any kind under the apparatus is not advisable for the following reasons:

(a) the mat may slip,
(b) the whole landing area may not be covered and so invite dangerous landings,
(c) a mat may give a child a false sense of security.'

2 Next, each group could have a form, wide side up. The children are encouraged to move across it, and along it from side to side, using the five jumps freely. The teacher develops different ways of going up, body shapes in the air, hands and feet working close together or far apart, ways of arriving and alighting on.

Great stress is next laid on how to *meet the floor*. Ways of spreading out and going on are explored, of landing low and bouncing on, and landing low and going on into a roll. Throughout, resilience in getting on to the feet again after an activity is an important point to emphasize.

When this is mastered, the class concentrates on how to get higher into the air; and then combines getting high into the air with meeting the floor.

3 At this point, group work can start with three groups working at getting over mats with rolls and three groups at moving across and along forms.

4 Further class activities can be developed, in subsequent lessons, using low apparatus such as rolled mats, spring boards, low beams,

wallbars, etc. To begin with getting on and off is stressed *before* there is any going *over* raised apparatus.

These further class activities can be built into the group work (see 3) in the same lessons as they develop, until the final stage is reached where each group has its own apparatus arrangement to work at. The challenge now may be either the same for all groups or differently worded to suit the apparatus set-up of each group, but in either case based on the lesson theme so that the children can apply the experience gained on the floor. Thus, the building up of the qualities required in the group work and the limitations which will occur there, will be coached in the earlier parts of the lesson, so that lessons will emerge in which the theme culminates in thoughtful and purposeful group activity.

To give the children confidence in the gymnasium and the apparatus, organization is advisable and reference should be made to Chapter 7 for suggestions on group numbers, placing of apparatus ready for group work, moving on to a new group place, use of work cards in helping each group to set up its own apparatus and to give the group task, group leaders, safety.

Group work arrangements are continued over a series of lessons, each group having a turn at two or three sets of apparatus in each lesson. At the start of group work, each group goes to the space for the apparatus for which they are responsible. With the help of their work cards, and under supervision, the apparatus is set up and checked by the teacher, who then moves the groups on to the places they are due to start from, following on the previous lesson. The arrangement of apparatus must, of course, remain the same until all the groups have been round once but then it should be subject to alteration because the work must be progressing as the children's ability develops. The same pattern of apparatus in continual use is an indictment of the teacher's observation and provision.

Thereafter, forms will be turned to narrow side up; one form will be placed on top of another; height of other apparatus will increase; sloping and angled surfaces will appear by hooking forms on to beams and wallbars; window ladders will come into use; ropes will be used to get on to and off beams, boxes, etc.; two kinds of apparatus will be arranged in conjunction or to provide a gap – e.g. beam and box, beating board and box.

Moving of Apparatus

The teacher should train the children so that all apparatus is put out noiselessly and with the right number of people carrying each piece. For example:

1 Forms – two to a form or even four if the children are small.

Forms to be lifted and never dragged. No standing on the cross bar in case of tipping.

2 Mats – four to a mat, one to each handle.

3 Beams – one to pull and one to steady the upright. Slow pulling down of the beam and no running underneath. Teacher to check the bolt, pegs and wedges.

4 Box – two to a lift, four to the padded top which is top-heavy, hands in the hand holds.

5 Horse and buck – two or four to each. The children should be taught how to adjust the height, and the bigger children should put them away adjusted back to the lower height ready for other classes.

Catching

Catching (supporting or standing by) has not been mentioned at the primary stage in gymnastics nor is it considered necessary in secondary work. Working with apparatus, the child demonstrates his ability to manage his body in a more demanding situation. The teaching in the primary school, and at the stage under discussion, has as a fundamental objective the development of body management. Tasks and arrangements of apparatus are both geared to the stage the children have reached in their attainment of this ability. Each child should therefore be capable of giving an answer, his own answer, to suit the limitations of the task set. Presumably, this answer will be in terms of individual ability to manage the body so the child should not need a catcher. If it is also in terms of individual inventiveness, how can the teacher anticipate and prepare to catch every child?

Progression

Once the children are working happily and safely with their new teacher in their new environment, and the teacher is confident of the basic elements of receiving weight and use of space and response from his class, further themes can be planned in schemes of work:

A. To Check Body Management Further

1 *Locomotion* with subordinate themes of Pathway, Direction and Level.

2 *Stillness* with subordinate themes of Bearing Weight and Transferring Weight.

3 *Transferring Weight to Adjacent Parts.*

4 *Transferring Weight to Non-Adjacent Parts.*

5 *Curling and Stretching.*

6 *Twisting and Turning.*

7 *Body Shape.*

8 *Flight.* It is important to stress this theme whilst the children are still light enough to experience propulsion into the air, as this makes gymnastics exciting and thus provokes enthusiasm.

9 *Symmetry and Asymmetry.*

10 *Balance and Off-balance.*

Note: The weight factor will be associated with all the above themes:

   (a) lightness or lack of tension in softly meeting the floor, especially in locomotion and flight,
   (b) use of energy and effort, especially in locomotion and flight,
   (c) control of effort and body weight throughout.

B. To Develop Relationships Further

(Those already made have been mainly with the floor and apparatus.) If the children have not previously experienced partner work, the teacher should begin at the beginning (see Chapter 8) and work through stages (i), (ii) and (iii) before proceeding to:

(iv) In contact with a partner.

   (a) Ways of supporting a partner.
   (b) Using ways of supporting, build up sequences in which partners travel.
   (c) Partners counterbalance each other's weight by grip or support.
   (d) Assisting a partner's flight.
   (e) One lifts, holds and lowers his partner with control. (A difficult task, only possible when the children have acquired considerable control of their own weight.)

(v) Work in threes.

   (a) Matching in three simultaneously.
   (b) Matching in cannon.
   (c) Complementary shapes or movements in three or two against one.
   (d) Working individually to produce a complementary pattern, rhythm or shape in movement.
   (e) Two assisting one, or one assisting two, in flight, swing, lift or catch. (A difficult task for an advanced class.)

Note: The weight factor is present here too, in control of own and partner's weight.

C. To Develop Quality Further

The four movement factors will have been evident in the themes already taken, but now that the children have some knowledge of working in a variety of ways, they can be stressed as main themes thus making them more meaningful.

1 Weight:

    (a) *Light and Heavy,*
    (b) *Pushing and Pulling,*
    (c) *Lifting and Lowering,*
    (d) *Gripping and Swinging.*

2 Space:

    (a) *Lifting a Part of the Body High,*
    (b) *Body Parts Meeting and Parting,*
    (c) *Movement Near the Body and Far Away,*
    (d) *Parts of the Body Leading a Movement.*

3 Time:

    (a) *Quick and Slow,*
    (b) *Variations of Speed, including Acceleration and Deceleration,*
    (c) *Movement with Momentum,*
    (d) *Rhythmic Phrases, alone and with a partner.*

4 Flow:

    (a) *Simultaneous Movement* – that is parts of the body moving at the same time,
    (b) *Successive Movement* – that is wave-like movement.

It is not intended to suggest ways of introducing these themes with appropriate tasks, as examples were given in the earlier chapters on primary school gymnastics. Rather is it expected that these will be referred to and adapted through the teacher's increased understanding and personal approach. The present-day method allows for the children's individuality; it would therefore seem logical to expect the teacher's personality and inventiveness also to be given full scope.

GAMES TRAINING

In the introduction to this chapter, it was pointed out that the child entering secondary education is no different from the same child who left the junior school a few weeks earlier. The summer holiday has made very little difference to his skill, stamina and physique. Indeed, the insecurity of the change-over may even result in a temporary lessening of his skill. A common argument in favour of major games at this stage, and even for juniors, is that the children want to play a proper game. Of course they do, but to *enjoy* a game the players must possess skill, otherwise all they achieve is frustration and a dislike for the experience which may be permanent. One school of thought recommends giving children a ball and the opportunity, and then leaving them to get on with their learning but, for the majority, games skills are rarely so natural that provision of opportunity is all that is needed for mastery.

Before he is given a grounding in the basic skills of many games, it is quite impossible to plunge the 11-year-old into playing any one full-scale major game. Apart from their skill content, such games also demand an amount of co-operative play that the child has not yet acquired, nor will he, unless he commences the secondary school with a planned and progressive scheme of games training designed to develop both his skill and relationships, through practices and simplified versions of a wider variety of games than is offered in most schools. The pride with which a school claims to be a 'football school' and boasts supremacy in the junior football league is a clear indication of its lack of educational principles. In the education of such young children, 'the' game is not the important thing; the general progress of the greatest number of children should be. The games programme must not cater for the few natural players at the expense of the many; it should rather aim at a wide range of skills and interests for all.

Aims

The aims of games training for the age group 11 to 13 years of age, should be:

(i) vigorous exercise for *all* the children,

(ii) intense satisfaction and enjoyment based on individual participation and increased personal skill,

(iii) a developing awareness of, and co-operation with, a partner, then a small group, so fostering team spirit,

(iv) increasing satisfaction in team play and the sacrifice of selfish, individualistic display of skill to the good of the 'team'.

These aims can be achieved by planning in two stages.

STAGE I: RECAPITULATION

It is essential to pick up the threads of the work done in the junior school in order to re-establish confidence in personal skill *and* to ensure a common background on which to base the development of the secondary games programme.

The reader should here refer back to the suggestions for primary games training made in Chapter 10.

Obviously, at the primary stage, each child enjoyed maximum access to the ball and as much of any 'game' as any other member of his group or 'team'. Thus on arrival in the secondary school each one should possess:

(a) general 'ball sense', the result of constantly handling balls of all sorts and sizes in a variety of ways calling for dexterity and anticipation, *viz.:* throwing, catching, bouncing, passing, striking, kicking, heading, batting, aiming;

(b) the ability to play, successfully, a number of group games; games which have skills in common with the major games but not the size of team or pitch, or the high degree of co-operative play required for the full-scale versions of such games.

For the first term or two, depending on the all-over standard and progress of the class, *schemes* of work can be based on the skill practices and small group games suggested for the 7 to 11 age group. In presenting the work, due regard must be given to:

(i) the need for adapting manner and method to the age of the children,

(ii) the fact that, whereas the primary child with his hunger for skill was content to practise such a skill incessantly as an end in itself, this is no longer so for the 11-year-old who needs to see the relevance and purpose of the skill. It is not enough for him that he can do a thing, it must be worth doing because it matches up with a partner's ability or outwits that of an opponent. The skill practised must therefore be applied to a 'games' situation as soon as possible, e.g. heading a ball will become more relevant when a partner is added to the practice; with opposition (pig in the middle) the challenge and satisfaction are increased even further. Linked with this is the fact that unless the individual is put in the games situation to co-operate and oppose, he may become so concerned with his personal skill that he will never make a good team player.

The time allocated will most probably be 45 minutes, and allowing time for completely changing and showering, this should leave about 35 minutes. With good preparation and organization, a most satisfactory period of vigorous activity is possible in such a time. The lesson can be planned in three parts as suggested for the primary stage:

1 *Introduction*

Warming up activities based on footwork and speed.

2 *Skill training*

Practices: individual, partner and in threes.

3 *Climax*

Application, of the skills practised, to a group game or simplified version of a minor game. 'Teams' should progress from the organization used for skill training to *two versus two, three versus three, four versus four, five versus five.*

STAGE II: FURTHER DEVELOPMENT OF GAMES PLAY

Now that the teacher has knowledge of the class as a whole and some indication of individual ability and potential, planning can be more progressive and more specialized, in that certain games can be concentrated on for a period of time such as a term. This also conveniently fits with the seasonal nature of games, so that those which are particularly warming and vigorous can be planned for a winter term, whereas games calling for finer and less vigorous skill, such as cricket, take place in the summer term.

The children, as they move up the school, come along to the lesson more and more intent on playing a game. Therefore, the teacher must return the skills and techniques to the games' context as quickly as possible. It is no good having so much practice of technique that there is none of the 35 minutes teaching time left in which to try it out; the practice is only relevant to the children if it has an outlet under what approximates to games conditions. The division of time between skill training and the game form is a matter of individual judgement but, as a general rule, the 'game' should occupy at least half of the lesson time. The teacher may choose to present the lesson in one of two ways:

Either

1 *Introduction*
2 *Skill Training*
3 *Game*, i.e. small teams playing on a number of small pitches, and/or *Relay races*

or

1 *Personal limbering with or without the relevant apparatus*
   Game, i.e. small teams playing on a number of small pitches
2 *Technique practices* and/or *Relay races*
3 *Return to the game*, as above.

Notes on Material for Lessons

1 *Introductory Work Under the First Plan*

The work should be based on footwork such as running fast (for speed), running slowly (for endurance and stamina), running and jumping (to reach high balls), running and turning (to keep up with the game), running and swerving (for dodging), dodging over lines, in and out of hoops, etc. (for attack and defence), jumps of all kinds and skipping with ropes (for strong agile feet and legs).

K

2 *Skill Training*

Individual, partner and small group skill practices should be taken either consecutively as class activities or simultaneously as group work.

Progression of small group from individual practices can develop in this way:

individual
partner $\Big\}$ – skill drills;

1 *versus* 2   – as in pig in the middle;
2 *v.*   2
3 *v.*   3 $\Big\}$ – as in team passing, kicking, hitting (hockey), etc.;
4 *v.*   4
5 *v.*   5   – suitable for simplified forms of minor and major games.

Choice of skill training practices under the first plan requires care to ensure the interest of the children.

Certain games lend themselves to the process of separating the basic skills from the game itself, e.g. netball provides a number of different passes which can be practised in pairs.

Such practices may, however, be too easy and thus fail to educe interest and effort, though, on the other hand, if too difficult, the practices may discourage the players. The teacher's knowledge of the class ability, gained in the recapitulation stage, is useful here in producing practices of a suitable standard. A standard just ahead of ability allows the teacher to let the children try the practice, then by simplifying it he can help them to feel progress and the achievement of the original task; a very satisfying experience.

There is another danger in breaking the skill down too small in that when it is put together again, the whole skill may not represent the separate parts which have been practised. This has often happened in the past, for instance, in the teaching of stick work in hockey and service and strokes in tennis.

Choice of technique practices under the alternative plan depends upon the teacher's careful observation of the game(s) at the beginning of the lesson. In preparation he will have picked out the techniques of the 'game' planned, listed the main coaching points needed to increase motor skill in each of these, and then devised appropriate practices ready for use. As the children play, the teacher will then be mentally registering, in order of priority, the techniques requiring practice. Stopping the game after a satisfactory 'go', the teacher should comment favourably and helpfully on the play, then point out one or two of the main techniques requiring practice to improve the standard. The children, then, readily accept the technique practices organized in the second part of the lesson and return to the game again with increased skill, and anxious to prove their ability.

Relevance of Practices. The object of the practice must be obvious to the children so that they can measure their immediate progress in the acquiring of skill, and also appreciate the relevance of the skill drill to the ultimate game (or form of game they are learning).

3 Game

It must be emphasized that in both the first and the alternative plan the word 'game' indicates small teams playing on a number of small pitches.

Choice should be based on as wide a range of skill as possible to cater for all tastes and interests. Schemes should also be progressive so that skill and co-operative play increase as more demands are made on the children by bigger teams, larger pitches, longer duration of play, more complex organization, stricter rules.

This kind of progression can be seen in the group and minor games developing eventually into e.g. netball:

TECHNIQUE PRACTICES

1 Passing big balls in pairs
2 With opposition – pig in the middle

Team passing in fours (2 *v.* 2)
in sixes (3 *v.* 3), etc.
Add a method of scoring (see Chapter 10)

Circle pass out
Add opposition

Captain ball

Dodge ball in threes (2 *v.* 1)
Circle dodge ball in fours or fives (1 or 2 in the middle)
Three court dodge ball in twelves (2 fours *v.* 1 four)

Post ball

Skittle ball

Netball

The particular skills of netball, such as shooting into a ring, could be practised previous to the term in which proper netball is to be introduced, the children meanwhile appreciating that their games training is leading to this game. It will be evident that the suggested progression could equally well lead up to basketball, with extra technique practices in dribbling and shooting.

Tennis and cricket could be similarly developed:

TECHNIQUE PRACTICES

1 Throwing and catching small balls
2 Bouncing and pat bouncing small balls
3 Striking small balls

Keeping the ball up in pairs (1 *v.* 1)
fours (2 *v.* 2), etc.

'Fives' against a wall

Padder tennis in pairs (1 *v.* 1)
fours (2 *v.* 2)

Hot rice

French cricket

Tip and run

Rounders in fours (batsman, bowler, backstop,
fielder and one base)
in sevens (full pitch but only one batsman
to prevent waiting to hit)

Stoolball

$\downarrow$

Cricket or tennis

From the practice of keeping the ball up in pairs and then fours, the game of volley ball could also be developed, by introducing a larger ball, such as a Frido ball, and a net for each small group.

Relay Races

These are suggested for occasional use in games training. The present, almost total, neglect is scarcely justified when one considers the appeal they have for children. They do not promote skill, as this tends to disintegrate in the excitement of the keen competition and quick climax, but they can be a means of training useful bursts of speed for most ball games, as well as for athletics. Most of the criticism levelled against relay races is the result of poor and unfair organization; in that teams are so big that too many children wait for turns in proportion to those being active, courses are inadequately defined, or the teacher fails to control boisterous and biased team feeling. Given small teams, eight teams of four children rather than four teams of eight, fun and stimulation result. Furthermore, children of poorer ability experience, in the quick climax of a relay race, an excitement and satisfaction rare to them, lacking as they do the co-operative play and sustained effort necessary to the enjoyment of team games.

Coaching

The children should be given time for a sensible amount of un-interrupted practice, but it is wrong to let them go on too long performing a skill incorrectly, lest the wrong way becomes habitual. The 'throw-up-in-front' style of service in tennis is one example which for many has persisted to the adult stage through lack of coaching.

Through his experience and the knowledge of others, the teacher is in a position to help the children to build up the techniques most appropriate to the equipment and purpose of the game under practice. Thus *coaching* aims to eliminate haphazard chance and helps to guarantee purposeful and productive play. The best coaching is positive, directing the practice so that skill becomes increasingly efficient.

Apparatus

The correct equipment should be used, whenever possible, in learning to play specific games. However, the importance of success breeding success in skill learning should be appreciated and, therefore, to persist with the use of hard balls in rounders practice, if fear of the impact reduces catching skill to a minimum, would be unproductive. It is much better in this situation to build up confidence in catching through using soft balls. A further example, in rounders, applies to the truncheon. It is the experience of the impact of the truncheon on the ball which breeds further skill in hitting. But few children get this experience with the narrow cylindrical truncheon, so it is sensible to practise, and play at first, with small cricket bats which present a wider and flat surface to the ball.

Rules

Books of rules, and information about pitches, equipment, coaching and umpiring, are easily available to teachers. There are now, for instance, over fifty books in the series 'Know the Game', many of them dealing with suitable minor and major games. Also the national bodies publish books of rules and coaching for the major games which they govern.

Summary

If the children, by the age of 13 or 14, have had a programme such as the one outlined, they should now be confident in the variety of their skill and able to try all the games and sports for which the school can provide teaching and facilities. Then follows the time for each child to choose and specialize.

SWIMMING

If the children have not already had an opportunity to learn to swim, it is most urgent that they be given this chance immediately, therefore swimming is included in the winter physical education programme and not left until the summer term at the end of their first year of secondary education. The children have an advantage which it is wise to make use of quickly, in that the proportion of fat to body bulk at this age is still high and therefore conducive to easy flotation. Unfortunately they lack the confidence in their own ability to swim, which would have come more easily at an earlier age, before their appreciation of fear developed, but this may be outweighed by their keenness to learn the new skill offered on promotion to the secondary school.

Facilities

As suggested in the introduction to the chapter, the facilities for swimming at this stage may be:

(i)   a learner pool on the school premises,

(ii) a traditional bath on the school premises,

(iii) use of the public baths.

Only in the case of facilities provided on the school premises is the non-specialist teacher likely to be responsible for swimming teaching. In one respect this may be an advantage, for the organization and control of activity is very much easier when the space is not shared by the general public. Use of the public baths usually involves the acceptance of teaching by the resident swimming instructor, in which case the teacher is responsible only for the children's changing and behaviour.

The suggestions made here are based on a school learner pool and the reader can adapt them to a school bath with a deep end. The learner pool is suggested to promote rapid progress in confidence for the reasons given in Chapter 11.

Aims

The aims of swimming teaching for the age group 11 to 13 must be:
  (a) to reinforce (further to primary teaching) or establish (if the children have not received instruction in the primary school) *confidence*, then
  (b) to promote *technique*.

An immediate objective, for the teacher, is to grade the children so that those who can already swim are not held back by the simple work necessary for the non-swimmers, and the latter are helped to progress and leave the 'beginner' stage as quickly as possible. In this way the teacher will benefit by having a more even standard from which to promote technique.

Depth of Water

Although the children are quite tall, they may be more fearful of the water than if they had been introduced to it at five years of age. In order to get them 'waterborne' as quickly as possible, water depth can commence at 2 feet with the object of increasing it as soon as possible to 3 to 5 feet.

Temperature

Water temperature can be as high as 80° F. at first, dropping as the whole class acquires the ability to keep warm by actually *swimming*. It is quite impossible to promote confidence in learners who are shivering both with fear and cold. If the children are warm and relaxed, confidence can be more easily developed.

Code of Conduct

The same strict code of conduct at the pool must be laid down for the secondary children as was suggested in Chapter 11 for the primary school. (See page 90.)

Artificial Aids

These are also discussed in Chapter 11 and, for the reasons given there, it is suggested that, to begin with, each child has an inflatable ring. Other aids, such as flippers for propulsion, may be used later as needed.

References in Chapter 11 to the teacher's manner and organization also apply here. The note on frequency of lessons is worth considering and might suggest to a school the idea of having 'daily lessons' in swimming for the first week or two in September. This intensive practice could give the 11-year-olds a 'flying start' in their swimming education, besides creating confidence helpful to their general progress in school.

Activity

Any of the following, suitably adapted and presented to the particular class, will promote *Confidence*:

(i) Sit down in a space – check spaces, as room to swim will always be important, so this is a good habit to develop.

(ii) Splash feet, then hands. Combine these and some children will immediately feel the 'upthrust' from the water and thus achieve buoyancy.

(iii) Lean back with weight on hands – splash feet again – bottoms will lift, supported by rings. Encourage those individuals ready for it to put heads further back until ears are in the water and go on splashing feet and legs upwards and downwards. By adding splashing of hands, some children will propel themselves backwards. There is no problem about getting up from this supine position as the water is so shallow.

(iv) In spaces, kneeling down facing the water and with hands flat on the floor of the pool. Push feet back so that legs are lifted and the whole body is on the water surface. 'Walk' on hands about the space, pushing up on to finger tips. Some children will take finger tips off and find themselves floating.

(v) Following walking on finger tips, develop 'dog paddling', encouraging the children to feel themselves 'pulling' (mental practice) on the water. A few children will instinctively splash their feet behind them and be actually 'swimming'.

(vi) Kneel in the water and splash it up on to the face with two hands. Encourage bending nearer to the water and, from this angle, most children will immerse the whole face in their enthusiasm. This is a much pleasanter experience than going under gradually, chin, mouth, nose, eyes, top of head; because at the point where the mouth is under and nose still free, the child can still breathe in and risks taking splashed up water too, which is rather painful. With both nose and mouth immersed simultaneously, it is impossible to breathe in, so the method of immersing the whole face is safer and pleasanter.

(vii) Practice immersion of face and opening eyes in the water by looking for and picking up coloured rings or discs, one for each child (see Chapter 11).

(viii) Holding hands in pairs, taking turns at 'ducking under'.

(ix) Holding the rail lying forward with face immersed, splashing legs. Repeat on the back.

(x) Hands joined in circles of eight, numbered in twos. Ones and twos lie back on the water alternately, the supports standing with feet firmly apart. Show, and coach, how to regain a standing position from back float by sweeping the arms firmly down towards the feet, bending the hips back and pushing the head as far forward as possible. This is much easier to learn and practise with the circle support.

(xi) Repeat the above practice with front float position. Show and coach recovery to standing by sweeping the arms back and drawing the knees up.

Technique

To develop strokes the teacher must consider which method to use:

1 Single stroke,
2 Multi-stroke.

These are discussed in Chapter 11 with suggestions for developing the various swimming strokes. It is not necessary to repeat these suggestions, but the teacher should take care to present the material appropriately for the 11-year-olds.

This is basically the same as for the primary children:

1 Confidence practices.
2 Technique practices.
   Individual, partner or group practice of push and glide, recovery, mushroom float, strokes, entry to the water.
3 Free practice.
   Strokes, entry to the water by jumping or diving, stunts.

L

Stroke Analysis

The teacher should refer to the A.S.A. and other handbooks for the analysis necessary to help him teach and coach style in strokes and diving.

Competition

Some means of measuring progress helps to promote swimming ability, but it is preferable to match each child against his own previous achievement rather than that of his taller or stronger peers. The teacher should devise class or school tests in terms of widths and lengths of the pool, and then promote the children to A.S.A. Survival Awards and Life Saving Tests.

Summary

The emphasis has been on making every child in the group a swimmer; obviously many of the children will have made great progress and should be swimming and diving really well. The teacher should have helped the latter group to achieve the highest possible standard, but the main purpose of this basic course is to cater for all.

DANCE

Dance, more than any other aspect of the physical education programme, exemplifies the work and philosophy of Rudolf Laban. The aims given by Laban to the teacher are:

1 To make the children conscious of the principles governing movement;
2 To awaken a broad outlook on human activities through observation of the flow of movement used;
3 To foster artistic expression;
4 To preserve spontaneity of movement.

All four aims are important for the age under consideration; the first two being equally applicable to the functional and skilful aspects of the physical education programme. Aim 3 emphasizes a point already made – the need to balance such a programme – and at no stage is the need greater for girls and boys to have opportunity for expressive movement. To aim at preserving spontaneity of movement is also necessary, for it is important to help the 11 to 15-year-olds to develop the ability to communicate in a lively and expressive way. This ability is closely linked with the developing personality and a vital factor in establishing relationships in preparation for contacts with the adult world.

Dance is easier to teach to the 5 to 11 age range as the younger children react more spontaneously, because the desire to move in a dance-like way is still alive. Also, the class teacher has contact with the children in other activities and can reinforce and integrate ideas, even if not specially trained in dance.

The secondary school teacher is probably a specialist but could well meet a difficult climate of opinion. The children's attitudes will vary; being drawn from a number of schools they will have different degrees of familiarity with dance and interest in it. Furthermore, their very different movement backgrounds will present a wide range of ability. Thus the content of the work must be such that all levels of interest and ability can achieve some enjoyment and success.

From the graph (Figure 8 on page 108) it can be seen that permutations of themes 11 to 14 form the matrix of lessons planned for the 11 to 15-year-olds. If there is no previous dance experience in this group the earlier themes would be introduced first to ensure a sound foundation and understanding of basic principles. The elementary themes must come in the first and second years together with those suited to the age groups 11 to 12 and 12 to 13.

The structure of the lesson follows the plan suggested in Chapter 4, examples of its adaptation to the dance lesson being given in the chapter on dance in primary education (Chapter 12). In fact, the reader should make full use of Chapter 12 for the necessary lesson material under the headings of language, effort actions, themes, accompaniment, stimuli and ideas. The plan should be as follows:

1 Warming and limbering,
2 Movement training,
3 Climax,
4 Unwind.

Each lesson should have a satisfying *climax*, a gathering together into a whole, a complete 'dance' based upon the appropriate themes. This dance could be in the form of a group dance, a study, or a dance drama. The latter has particular appeal for the boys at this stage as it can involve them in strong dynamic action. The girls too enjoy this experience but also need opportunities to indulge their liking for lyrical dance.

Accompaniment for dance for the 11 to 15 age group must at first be at a level which the children know and accept. This usually implies music which is strong and rhythmic. Success could lead to the use of less familiar music.

The 13-year-olds, particularly the girls, are ready for directed movement. Some experience of effort actions in relation to the effort cube will give opportunity for practising effort transition within a specific spatial orientation, and for developing rhythmic sequences of disciplined shape and pattern. This is the time for the teacher to choreograph complete dances based upon shapes and efforts, where individual technical ability is called upon. The girls at this stage are specially critical of their own performance and that of the other girls in the class, thus the need to train observation and develop it to help one another should not be overlooked.

The 14 to 15-year-olds still feel the need for a great deal of direction. The emotional strains of adolescence are a stumbling-block to the creative side of work at this stage. This may explain why the desire to perform set dances and to improve personal performance is so strong. Thus 13 to 15 is the age range for which folk and national dance, with their clarity of pattern and rhythm, have maximum appeal. A wise teacher will recognise the symptoms and provide these attractions, without their limitations, until the creative urge returns at 16 to 18 years.

Social dance is valuable to the adolescent, if well taught and based on the ability to move well and appreciate the pattern and rhythm of creative dance. All types, *folk, national, ballroom*, prove most acceptable to secondary children if taught to mixed groups and out of school hours in a society or club. Added value lies in the children's appreciation of entrance into an adult activity.

ATHLETICS

There are two reasons for including athletics in the basic programme of physical education in the secondary school:

(a) Athletic activity is part of the child's natural movement and has been developing throughout his primary education.

(b) Athletic training promotes healthy physical development because it involves whole body action and takes place in the fresh air out of doors.

Thus, the purpose of the training is educational, in that it fits into the child's general movement education and is concerned with his natural physical development. The purpose is *not* to train the few for competition, but to give all children the benefit of healthy and interesting activity for which each has a natural bent.

Simplified, athletic activity separates into three types:

    (i)   Running,

    (ii) Throwing,

    (iii) Jumping.

If the reader considers the primary programme, it will be obvious that all three have been catered for and developed. All that is necessary, in the two years under consideration, is to begin applying the skills acquired to particular situations and apparatus.

In the early part of this chapter, the suggestion was made that two periods per week be allocated to athletics in the summer term. This indicates that the lessons take place out of doors on the school field. The space needed is therefore available and the teacher can choose the most suitable areas and surfaces to mark out appropriately for the different practices.

Specialization

At this stage specialization should not occur. Consistent with the policy of giving the children a wide range of skills during the basic course in the secondary school, the work should be of a general nature including all three types of athletic activity.

Timing

Allowing time for changing and showering from the usual 45-minute lesson, the teacher will have approximately 35 minutes left for teaching. With good preparation and organization, this should be adequate for an active and enjoyable session.

Changing

The children should change completely into vest and shorts with the addition of a warm sweater, to wear until they are limbered and warm. Special shoes are not necessary at this stage providing the children have pliable sandshoes, securely laced.

The lesson should follow the same development of limbering, training and application, as for other forms of physical education.

1 *Introduction*

    (a) Limbering by self-chosen practices until the whole class is assembled.

    (b) Teacher-directed activity on the lines of running fast and shuttle runs (for speed in sprints), running slowly (for stamina in long-distance runs), running and jumping (for take-off), skipping with ropes (for strong, agile feet and legs).

2 *Training*

The basic skills of the various athletic events can be introduced as class activities, that is, probably two or three practices in succession giving a variety of activity.

Thus in one lesson, the teacher could teach and give practice and coaching for:

    (i) Sprint start,

(ii) Throwing balls (tennis balls) for distance,

(iii) Scissor kick.

3 Climax

The training already given can be developed in the form of group work, following the organization set up in the gymnastic lesson. From the three practices suggested above, group work might consist of:

(i) Two groups working separately on sprint starts over a marked distance. In each group one child can take turns at being the starter.

(ii) Two groups working separately on throwing for distance.

(iii) Two groups working separately on developing scissor kick, off either foot, over canes on skittles.

In succeeding lessons, further skills can be taught and built into the group work so as to increase variety and progress the activity. Apparatus, too, should progress in interest, height, weight, etc.

Organization

The arrangements and organization of the activities in the space is vital to the children's safety, especially for throwing events when such equipment as canes may be substituted to prepare for using javelins.

The teacher should refer to the A.A.A. and other handbooks for details of athletic techniques, coaching, equipment and tracks.

Summary

After two summer terms of athletic activity developing along these lines, the 13-year-old should be ready to specialize and compete in the events for which he now shows particular aptitude.

Chapter 15

The Teacher – Educational Effects of Physical Education – Transfer of Training

THE TEACHER

One of the functions of a school is to concern itself with the children's health, and physical education is part of this provision. However, it must constantly be borne in mind that there is no profitable part of education that is solely physical. In the same way we cannot isolate intellectual or moral education. Thus health is not judged on the study of physical well-being alone.

It is assumed that the teacher has a conception of health as that state of body and mind which enables the individual to bring to all activities feelings of interest, efficiency, determination and happiness. This ideal of health is not just freedom from ailments and obvious deformities. It is the realization, in each individual, of his highest physical and mental possibilities.

All the work of the school should contribute to this end; but physical education, in its modern form and most comprehensive sense, can and should have a major part to play in promoting the total health of every child.

One sign of normal health is that exercise is stimulating and pleasurable. With children's inborn pleasure in movement to help him, the teacher's work should not be difficult. Enjoyment and interest do not, however, depend on the work being a 'soft option' and without effort, for a good deal of the satisfaction lies in the chance the individual has to pit himself against and to meet challenge with a fair degree of success. Too much success indicates that the teacher has chosen work that is too easy, and too little that the work is too difficult, and in either case interest dies through lack of stimulation. This is why the work is planned, not to make a uniform demand on the whole class, but to allow for individual differences and varying contributions.

It is an immense advantage that the teacher has himself taken part in stimulating physical education lessons as a class member. The work done at school, during training, and also, perhaps, later in teachers' classes, should give him the 'feel' of the movement, as for instance, the kind of effort needed in body twisting, the skill of controlling the ball in a game, the appropriate response to the beat of a tambour.

Teachers' classes and holiday courses, apart from supplying fresh ideas so that the practising teacher is abreast of changing views and opinion, also keep him in touch with the children by enabling him to live again the experience of working in a class. They help him to remember how success or lack of it feels from the learner's point of view, and convince him of the importance of ensuring pleasure for every child in effortful activity and in achieving some feeling of mastery.

EDUCATIONAL EFFECTS OF PHYSICAL EDUCATION

It is unquestionable that the benefits of physical education are wider than its immediate and physiological effects. Nevertheless, too much has been claimed on the mental and moral side as an *inevitable* result of taking part in good gymnastics and well-taught games. Individuals, who in their games are honest, modest and considerate for others, do not necessarily reveal these same qualities in everyday life. A child who has learnt to co-operate in a team game will not, as a matter of course, co-operate readily in all social and community affairs; though he is likely to in other team games, having formed a habit response to such situations. This is analogous to the child who has formed a habit of tidiness and is tidy at school, but remains untidy at home or in public buildings and parks or on a picnic.

Habits are specific, and so long as a child conducts himself in a satisfactory way only in the playground or on the playing field, but does not realize that such behaviour is desirable and worthwhile in all departments of life, the mental and moral value of his physical education will be very restricted. This is obvious even in purely physical directions, in that the child may adopt a good posture during physical education lessons but a very poor one during the rest of the school day.

TRANSFER OF TRAINING

Transfer of training is not automatic. Habit training, though necessary in physical education, is not sufficient. It is only with the help of adults that the child will realize that many of the qualities connected with physical education are the very qualities valued in the good citizen. The teacher must not assume that the habits developed, for example fair play, taking turns, abiding by the umpire's decision, taking a share in moving apparatus, will function automatically. To ensure transfer of training there must be co-operation between the teacher of physical education and the rest of the staff in the deliberate fostering of ideals of behaviour. Then the boy or girl will realize that the demands made by an adult community are similar to those made by a team at school.

At the primary stage, the school tone will help the children to build up good habits of conduct and health, such as that windows should be opened, that people should share and co-operate, that authority is reasonable and trustworthy. As children reach the secondary school and adolescence, they can be guided to form what are technically named *sentiments and ideals*, that is they can be led to feel for themselves that such things as appearance, honesty, co-operation are to be cultivated for the well-being of the individual and the community. Such emotional conviction will do much to facilitate and ensure transfer of training from physical education to other spheres of activity in life.

List of Reference Books

GENERAL PHYSICAL EDUCATION

BILBROUGH and JONES. *Physical Education in the Primary School,* University of London Press, 1963

CAMERON AND CAMERON. *Education in Movement in the Infant School,* Blackwell, 1970

COPE, J. *Discovery Methods in Physical Education,* Nelson, Oct. 1967

D.E.S. *Moving and Growing, Physical Education in Primary Schools, Part I,* H.M.S.O., 1952

INNER LONDON EDUCATION AUTHORITY. *Movement Education for Infants,* I.L.E.A., 1963

SCHOOLS COUNCIL. *Physical Education 8–13,* Schools Council Working Paper 37

THACKRAY, R. M. *Music and Physical Education,* Novello, Second revised edition 1971

MOVEMENT

JORDAN, DIANA. *Childhood and Movement,* Blackwell, 1970

LOWNDES, BETTY. *Movement and Drama in the Primary School,* Batsford, 1971

NORTH, MARION. *A Simple Guide to Movement Teaching,* North, 1961

NORTH, MARION. *Composing Movement Sequences,* North, 1965

RANDALL, MARJORIE. *Basic Movement,* G. Bell and Sons, 1961

REDFERN, BETTY. *Introducing Laban Art of Movement,* Macdonald and Evans, Jan. 1965

WILES, JOHN and GARRARD, ALAN. *Leap to Life,* Chatto and Windus, 1951

GYMNASTICS

BUCKLAND, DON. *Activity in the Primary School: Gymnastics,* Heinemann, 1969

CAMERON AND PLEASANCE. *Education in Movement: School Gymnastics,* Blackwell, Revised edition 1971

INNER LONDON EDUCATION AUTHORITY. *Educational Gymnastics,* I.L.E.A., 1965

MAULDON and LAYSON. *Teaching Gymnastics*, Macdonald and Evans, Sept. 1965

MORISON, RUTH. *A Movement Approach to Educational Gymnastics*, I. M. Marsh College, 1960, Dent, 1969

PHYSICAL EDUCATION ASSOCIATION. *A Survey of Climbing Apparatus: An Analysis and Guide*, 25p (p. & p. 6p) from P.E.A., 10 Nottingham Place, London W1M 4AX

DANCE

CARROLL AND LOFTHOUSE. *Creative Dance for Boys*, Macdonald and Evans, 1969

GOODRIDGE, JANET. *Activity in the Primary School: Drama*, Heinemann 1970

LOFTHOUSE, P. *Activity in the Primary School: Dance*, Heinemann 1970

PRESTON DUNLOP, VALERIE. *A Handbook for Modern Educational Dance*, Macdonald and Evans, 1963

RUSSELL, JOAN. *Modern Dance in Education*, Macdonald and Evans, 1958

RUSSELL, JOAN. *Creative Dance in the Primary School*, Macdonald and Evans, Sept. 1965

SOCIETY FOR INTERNATIONAL FOLK DANCING. *European Folk Dances, Books 1, 2 and 3*, S.I.F.D., 1966

THACKRAY, R. M., *Music for Modern Educational Dance, Books 1, 2, 3, 4, 5 and 6*, Novello, n.d.

WIGMAN, MARY. *The Language of Dance*, Macdonald and Evans, Sept. 1966

GAMES AND ATHLETICS

ALL ENGLAND NETBALL ASSOCIATION. *An Introduction to Netball*, A.E.N.A., 1968

BAGGALLAY. *Netball for Schools*, Pelham Books, 1966

BLAXLAND. *Suggestions for Coaching Elementary Hockey*, Marjorie Pollard Publications, Oxford, 1968

DUNN, MARGARET. *Games Activities for Juniors*, Blackie, 1971

EDMUNDSON AND BURNUP. *Athletics for Boys and Girls*, G. Bell and Sons, 1971

FRITH AND LOBLEY. *Playground Games and Skills*, A. and C. Black, 1971

JOHNSON AND TREVOR. *A Suggested Games Scheme for Juniors*, Blackwell, 1970

KNOW THE GAMES SERIES, various titles, E.P. Publishing Co.

MAULDON AND REDFERN. *Games Teaching*, Macdonald and Evans, 1969

MESURIER, J. *Improve Your Athletics: 1. Track Events, 2. Field Events*, Penguin, 1968

NATIONAL ROUNDERS ASSOCIATION. *Coaching of the Game of Rounders*, N.R.A., 1957

Official Rules of Sports and Games 1972/73, Kaye and Ward, 1972

WISE, W. *Activity in the Primary School: Games and Sports*, Heinemann, 1970

WOODESON, P. J. and WATTS, D. *Schoolgirl Athletics*, S. Paul, Jan. 1966

SWIMMING

AMATEUR SWIMMING ASSOCIATION. *Swimming Instruction*, Educational Productions Publishing Co., 1963

ELKINGTON, HELEN. *Swimming with the Post*, Bristol Evening Post, Silver Street, Bristol

GIBSON, WINIFRED. *Shallow Water Method of Swimming Instruction*, Pitman, 1946

HOWARD, H. V. and GRAINGER, D. P. *Get Swimming*, Souvenir Press, July 1966

MORRIS, D. W. *Activity in the Primary School: Swimming*, Heinemann, 1971

NEWMAN, VIRGINIA HUNT. *Teaching an Infant to Swim*, Angus and Robertson, April 1968

RACKHAM, GEORGE. *Synchronized Swimming*, Faber and Faber, 1969

SARSFIELD, NORMAN W. *Swimming for Everyone*, Faber and Faber, June 1965

WHITING, H. T. A. *Teaching the Persistent Non-Swimmer*, G. Bell and Sons, 1970

EDUCATION

FROEBEL, F. *Education of Man*, Appleton, 1897

GESELL, A. and ILG, F.L. *The Child from Five to Ten*, Hamilton, 1965

List of Equipment Manufacturers

Olympic Gymnasium Co. Ltd, Olympic Works, Great Suffolk Street, London S.E.1.

R. W. Whittle, Ltd, P.V. Works, Monton, Eccles, Manchester.

Wicksteeds of Royston Ltd, Meridian Works, Barkway Road, Royston, Herts.

Index

Accidents, 127–8
Actions – five basic, 101
Activity method, 18
Agility, 30, 69
Aims, 13, 17, 143, 154
Analysis
  individual efforts, 19, 32
  movement, 22–4, 57, 60
  swimming strokes, 97, 154
Apparatus
  large, 43–50, 53
  organization and training, 31, 42, 53–4, 58, 74–5, 84, 139
  primary school games, 72, 83
  secondary school games, 149–50
  small, 42–5, 49, 53
  suitability, 31
Application
  movement, 16
  principles, 18
Approach
  child's 18
  conversational, 18
  informal, 18
  present-day, 18, 30, 71
  swimming, 90
  teacher's, 13
Asymmetry, 59, 61, 102
Athletics, 22, 156–8
  techniques, 158
Awareness
  body, 24, 33, 59, 101, 105
  dynamic, 103–5
  spatial, 102–3, 105

Balance, 39, 59
  off-balance, 40, 59
Body
  management, 2, 31–3, 140
  patches, 59
  points, 59
  shape, 24, 39, 58, 102, 137
Body weight
  bearing, 32, 38, 59

receiving, 32, 38, 136
transferring, 32, 38, 101
Buoyancy, 87, 89, 93

Catching – in gymnastics, 140
Challenge, 18, 22, 32
Changing for physical activity, 27, 72, 157
Class activity, 41–2, 48
Climax
  lesson, 27
  gymnastics lesson, 52–6
  games lesson, 80–1
  dance lesson, 155
Clothing for physical activity, 28, 135
Coaching, 19, 119–20, 149
Competition, 65, 82, 85, 154
Confidence, 16, 22, 139
  swimming, 90, 95, 152
Continuity
  follow on of lesson, 121, 135
  of movement, 59, 121
Contrast
  in partner work, 61
  teaching by, 37, 127

Dance, 22, 26
  accompaniment, 115, 155
  drama, 25, 115
  imagery, 113
  in primary education, 100
  in secondary education, 154–6
  social, 156
Demonstration
  child's, 19, 123–5
  teacher's, 19, 124
  value of, 125–6
Dimensional cross, 102
Direction of movement, 24
Discipline, 121
Drama, 25

Educational effects, 159–60

Effort, 103–4
  actions, 104
  cube, 102, 155
  the child's, 18, 19, 122
Elevation, 101
Enjoyment, 17, 36, 143
Exemption from physical education, 128
Exercise, 17, 143
Exploration, 16, 22, 30, 34–5
Expression, 17, 22
  self, 17, 109

Facilities
  primary school, 28–9, 30, 72, 73
  secondary school, 131
  swimming, 87–8, 150–1
First aid, 128
Flight, 40, 58, 141
Floor training, 31, 38, 43, 61, 136
Flow, 24, 25, 136
Free practice, 35–6, 136

Games, 22
  basic skills, 71, 75, 83, 143–4
  in primary education, 70–85
  in secondary education, 142–50
  major, 70–1, 85, 143
  minor, 84
  rules, 84, 150
  technique, 81–5, 146–9
  training, 26, 71–2
Group
  leaders, 54–5
  practices, 52–6, 137
  work, 49, 137–9
Gymnastics, 22, 26
  in the primary programme, 30–62
  in the secondary programme, 135–42
Health, 123, 159
Healthy attitude, 72
Hygiene of swimming, 90–1, 92

Icosahedron, 102
Individual
  child, 18
  differences, 14, 18, 97
Informality, 18

Integration, 20, 155

Jumps, 40, 58, 75, 79, 101, 137, 145
  five basic, 40, 58, 101, 137

Laban, Rudolf, 22, 101, 154
Landings, 40, 41, 58, 137, 138
Language
  body, 16
  of dance, 101, 109
Learner pools, 87
  depth of water, 87, 91, 151
  temperature of water, 88, 91, 151
Learning
  situation, 17
  stages, 16
  ways of, 16, 133–4
Lesson
  length, 27
  notes, 20–1
  plan, 27
Levels of movement, 24, 36
Limbering, 36, 75, 157
Limitations, 21, 32
Locomotion, 32, 37, 101

Manner – teacher's, 19, 90, 120
Mats – use of, 138
Mobility, 17
Movement
  axes of, 103
  contrasting, 37, 61
  creating, 16
  creative, 22
  expressive, 25, 154
  factors, 24, 141
  functional, 25
  ideas, 60, 114
  matching, 61
  memory, 60
  potential, 15, 69
  principles, 22, 24, 25, 154
  qualities, 36
  quality, 126, 141–2
  sentences, 110
  sequences, 59–60

Needs – children's, 13, 134–5

Observation, 19, 20, 32, 121–3
Octahedron, 102
Organization
  of apparatus, 20
  of group work, 20

Pace – the child's own, 18
Partner work, 61–2, 79, 95, 98
Path, pathways, 24, 36
Patterns
  air, 103
  floor, 37, 75, 103
Personality – development, 13
Percussion instruments, 104, 115,
  160
Physique, 17
Planes of movement, 102
Play, 16, 17, 70
  theories, 63–8
  values, 68–9
Posture, 14, 129
Preparation
  of body for action, 59
  of space, 28, 73
  of work, 20
Programme
  primary, 26–116
  secondary, 130–58
Progression, 18, 51, 57, 61, 62, 127,
  140
  of basic games skills, 75–80
  of group work, 49–50
  of sixteen basic movement
    themes, 108
Propulsion, 40

Quality of movement, 60–1

Races
  all-in, 81
  relay, 149
Readiness to learn, 79, 87
Recovery – of body after action, 59
Relationships, 26, 53, 116, 141, 154
  of parts of the body, 36
  with space, 37
Repetition, 16, 21, 64
Resilience, 40
Response, 19, 30

Rocking, 39, 40, 137
Rolling, 39, 61, 136–8
Rules – in games, 81, 84, 147, 150

Safety, 19, 28, 30, 31, 38, 40, 55–6,
  73, 158
Scheme of work, 20, 144
Scope
  of physical education, 22
  of the secondary programme,
    130–1
  widening of, 26, 130
Seasonal activity, 72, 145
Selection of movement, 16
Shallow water method, 91
Scoring, 80, 82
Skills
  acquisition, 17
  basic games, 71, 75, 83, 143–4
  maturation, 17, 71, 81
  motor, 17
  natural, 17
Space
  factor, 24
  general, 24, 101
  personal, 24
Spacing – free, 18, 30
Spring, 40
Stance in games, 78, 82
Standard of work, 126
Stillness, 59, 101
Stimuli in dance, 19, 109
Swimming, 22, 26
  artificial aids, 92, 94, 95, 97, 152
  awards, 97, 154
  code of conduct, 90, 152
  diving, 98, 154
  entry to the water, 92, 97
  frequency of lessons, 90
  in primary education, 86–99
  in secondary education, 150–4
  land drill, 99
  multi-stroke teaching method, 96,
    153
  single stroke teaching method,
    96, 153
  stroke analysis, 97, 154
  technique, 95, 96, 153
  values, 86, 99

Symmetry, 59, 61, 102

Take off, 40
Tasks, 18, 32, 119
Teaching technique, 18, 32, 117–29
Themes
  for lessons, 20, 60, 113, 140
  sixteen basic for dance, 105, 155
Time factor, 24
Timetabling physical education, 26–7, 82–3, 90, 132
Travelling about the space, 37, 60

Training
  social, 17, 27, 52
  transfer of, 160–1

Vocabulary of movement, 18, 33
Voice, 19, 119

Waiting for turns, 18
Weight
  factor, 24
  on hands, 41
Whistle – use of, 73, 89